FAVORITE BRAND NAME™

Low-Carb

RECIPES

Publications International, Ltd.

Favorite Brand Name Recipes at www.fbnr.com

Pictured on the front cover: Pork Chop Paprikash *(page 180)*.
Pictured on the back cover *(top to bottom):* Quick Orange Chicken *(page 158)* and Strawberry-Topped Cheesecake Cups *(page 306)*.

ISBN: 0-7853-9905-4

Library of Congress Control Number: 2004102737

Manufactured in China.

8 7 6 5 4 3 2 1

Nutritional Analysis: The nutritional information that appears with each recipe was submitted in part by the participating companies and associations. Every effort has been made to check the accuracy of these numbers. However, because numerous variables account for a wide range of values for certain foods, nutritive analyses in this book should be considered approximate.

Microwave Cooking: Microwave ovens vary in wattage. Use the cooking times as guidelines and check for doneness before adding more time.

Preparation/Cooking Times: Preparation times are based on the approximate amount of time required to assemble the recipe before cooking, baking, chilling or serving. These times include preparation steps such as measuring, chopping and mixing. The fact that some preparations and cooking can be done simultaneously is taken into account. Preparation of optional ingredients and serving suggestions is not included.

Contents

Starters

Peppered Shrimp Skewers

Makes 16 servings

⅓ **cup teriyaki sauce**
⅓ **cup ketchup**
2 **tablespoons dry sherry or water**
2 **tablespoons reduced-fat peanut butter**
1 **teaspoon hot pepper sauce**
¼ **teaspoon ground ginger**
32 **fresh large shrimp (about 1½ pounds)**
2 **large yellow bell peppers**
32 **fresh sugar snap peas, trimmed**

1. Coat rack of broiler pan with nonstick cooking spray; set aside.

2. Combine teriyaki sauce, ketchup, sherry, peanut butter, pepper sauce and ginger in small saucepan. Bring to a boil, stirring constantly. Reduce heat to low; simmer, uncovered, 1 minute. Remove from heat; set aside.

3. Peel and devein shrimp, leaving tails intact.

4. Cut each bell pepper lengthwise into 4 quarters; remove stems and seeds. Cut each quarter crosswise into 4 equal pieces. Thread 2 shrimp, 2 bell pepper pieces and 2 sugar snap peas onto each skewer*; place on prepared broiler pan. Brush with teriyaki sauce mixture.

5. Broil, 4 inches from heat, 3 minutes; turn. Brush with teriyaki sauce mixture; broil 2 minutes longer or until shrimp turn pink. Discard any remaining teriyaki sauce mixture. Transfer skewers to serving plates; garnish, if desired.

If using wooden skewers, soak in water 20 to 30 minutes before using to prevent burning.

Nutrients per Serving:
Calories: 69 (16% of calories from fat), Carbohydrate: 6g, Total Fat: 1g, Protein: 8g, Cholesterol: 66mg, Sodium: 258mg, Fiber: 1g

Peppered Shrimp Skewer

Cold Asparagus with Lemon-Mustard Dressing

Makes 2 appetizer servings

12 fresh asparagus spears
2 tablespoons fat-free mayonnaise
1 tablespoon sweet brown mustard
1 tablespoon fresh lemon juice
1 teaspoon grated lemon peel, divided

1. Steam asparagus until crisp-tender and bright green; immediately drain and rinse under cold water. Cover and refrigerate until chilled.

2. Combine mayonnaise, mustard and lemon juice in small bowl; blend well. Stir in ½ teaspoon lemon peel; set aside.

3. Divide asparagus between 2 plates. Spoon 2 tablespoons dressing over top of each serving; sprinkle each with ¼ teaspoon lemon peel. Garnish with carrot strips and edible flowers, such as pansies, violets or nasturtiums, if desired.

Nutrients per Serving:
Calories: 39 (14% of calories from fat), Carbohydrate: 7g, Total Fat: 1g, Protein: 3g, Cholesterol: 0mg, Sodium: 294mg, Fiber: 2g

Food Fact

The size of the asparagus stalk has no relationship to tenderness. Whether thick or thin, select asparagus with firm, straight stalks. Also, always choose asparagus stalks that show the most green color.

Mini Marinated Beef Skewers

Makes 6 servings (3 skewers each)

> 1 beef top round steak (about 1 pound)
> 2 tablespoons reduced-sodium soy sauce
> 1 tablespoon dry sherry
> 1 teaspoon dark sesame oil
> 2 cloves garlic, minced
> 18 cherry tomatoes (optional)

1. Cut beef crosswise into ⅛-inch slices. Place in large resealable plastic food storage bag. Combine soy sauce, sherry, oil and garlic in cup; pour over steak. Seal bag; turn to coat. Marinate in refrigerator at least 30 minutes or up to 2 hours.

2. Soak 18 (6-inch) wooden skewers in water 20 minutes.

3. Drain steak; discard marinade. Weave beef accordion-style onto skewers. Place on rack of broiler pan.

4. Broil 4 to 5 inches from heat 2 minutes. Turn skewers over; broil 2 minutes or until beef is barely pink.

5. If desired, garnish each skewer with 1 cherry tomato. Place skewers on lettuce-lined platter. Serve warm.

Nutrients per Serving:
Calories: 120 (30% of calories from fat), Carbohydrate: 2g, Total Fat: 4g, Protein: 20g, Cholesterol: 60mg, Sodium: 99mg, Fiber: <1g

Crab Canapés
Makes 16 servings

⅔ **cup fat-free cream cheese, softened**
2 **teaspoons lemon juice**
1 **teaspoon hot pepper sauce**
1 **package (8 ounces) imitation crabmeat or lobster, flaked**
⅓ **cup chopped red bell pepper**
2 **green onions with tops, sliced (about ¼ cup)**
64 **cucumber slices (about 2½ medium cucumbers cut into ⅜-inch-thick slices) or melba toast rounds**
Fresh parsley, for garnish (optional)

1. Combine cream cheese, lemon juice and hot pepper sauce in medium bowl; mix well. Stir in crabmeat, bell pepper and green onions; cover. Chill until ready to serve.

2. When ready to serve, spoon 1½ teaspoons crabmeat mixture onto each cucumber slice. Place on serving plate; garnish with parsley, if desired.

Tip: To allow flavors to blend, chill crab mixture at least 1 hour before spreading onto cucumbers or melba toast rounds.

Nutrients per Serving:
Calories: 31 (8% of calories from fat), Carbohydrate: 4g, Total Fat: <1g, Protein: 4g, Cholesterol: 5mg, Sodium: 178mg, Fiber: <1g

Baked Spinach Balls

Makes 12 servings

2 cups sage and onion or herb-seasoned bread stuffing mix
2 tablespoons grated Parmesan cheese
1 small onion, chopped
1 clove garlic, minced
¼ teaspoon dried thyme leaves
¼ teaspoon black pepper
1 package (10 ounces) frozen chopped spinach, thawed and well drained
¼ cup fat-free reduced-sodium chicken broth
2 egg whites, beaten
    Dijon or honey mustard (optional)

1. Combine bread stuffing mix, cheese, onion, garlic, thyme and pepper in medium bowl; mix well. Combine spinach, broth and egg whites in separate medium bowl; mix well. Stir into stuffing mixture. Cover; refrigerate mixture 1 hour or until firm.

2. Preheat oven to 350°F. Shape mixture into 24 balls. Place on ungreased baking sheet; bake spinach balls 15 minutes or until browned. Serve with mustard for dipping, if desired. Garnish, if desired.

Nutrients per Serving:
Calories: 52 (12% of calories from fat), Carbohydrate: 9g, Total Fat: 1g, Protein: 3g, Cholesterol: 1mg, Sodium: 227mg, Fiber: <1g

Chilled Shrimp with Chinese Mustard Sauce

Makes 6 servings

   1 cup water
   ½ cup dry white wine
   2 tablespoons reduced-sodium soy sauce
   ½ teaspoon Szechuan or black peppercorns
   1 pound raw large shrimp, peeled and deveined
   ¼ cup prepared sweet-and-sour sauce
   2 teaspoons hot Chinese mustard

1. Combine water, wine, soy sauce and peppercorns in medium saucepan. Bring to a boil over high heat. Add shrimp; reduce heat to medium. Cover and simmer 2 to 3 minutes or until shrimp are opaque. Drain well. Cover and refrigerate until chilled.

2. Combine sweet-and-sour sauce and mustard in small bowl; mix well. Serve as a dipping sauce for shrimp.

Health Note: Shellfish, such as shrimp, is an excellent source of low-calorie, low-fat protein. It's also rich in the minerals iron, copper and zinc, yet low in sodium.

Nutrients per Serving:
Calories: 92 (7% of calories from fat), Carbohydrate: 5g, Total Fat: 1g, Protein: 13g, Cholesterol: 116mg, Sodium: 365mg, Fiber: <1g

Easiest Three-Cheese Fondue

Makes 8 (3-tablespoon) servings

 1 tablespoon margarine
 ¼ cup finely chopped onion
 2 cloves garlic, minced
 1 tablespoon all-purpose flour
 ¾ cup reduced-fat (2%) milk
 2 cups (8 ounces) shredded mild or sharp Cheddar cheese
 1 package (3 ounces) cream cheese, cut into cubes
 ½ cup (2 ounces) crumbled blue cheese
 ⅛ teaspoon ground red pepper
 4 to 6 drops hot pepper sauce
   Breadsticks and assorted fresh vegetables for dipping

1. Heat margarine in small saucepan over medium heat until melted. Add onion and garlic; cook and stir 2 to 3 minutes or until tender. Stir in flour; cook 2 minutes, stirring constantly.

2. Stir milk into saucepan; bring to a boil. Boil, stirring constantly, about 1 minute or until thickened. Reduce heat to low; add cheeses, stirring until melted. Stir in red pepper and pepper sauce. Pour fondue into serving dish. Serve with dippers.

Lighten Up: To lower the total fat, use reduced-fat Cheddar cheese and cream cheese.

Nutrients per Serving:
Calories: 207 (74% of calories from fat), Carbohydrate: 3g, Total Fat: 17g, Protein: 10g, Cholesterol: 48mg, Sodium: 334mg, Fiber: <1g

Black Bean Quesadillas

Makes 8 servings

Nonstick cooking spray
4 (8-inch) flour tortillas
¾ cup (3 ounces) shredded reduced-fat Monterey Jack or Cheddar cheese
½ cup canned black beans, rinsed and drained
2 green onions with tops, sliced
¼ cup chopped fresh cilantro
½ teaspoon ground cumin
½ cup salsa
2 tablespoons plus 2 teaspoons fat-free sour cream
Chopped fresh cilantro, for garnish (optional)

1. Preheat oven to 450°F. Spray large nonstick baking sheet with nonstick cooking spray. Place 2 tortillas on prepared baking sheet; sprinkle each with half the cheese.

2. Combine beans, green onions, cilantro and cumin in small bowl; mix lightly. Spoon bean mixture evenly over cheese; top with remaining tortillas. Spray tops with cooking spray.

3. Bake 10 to 12 minutes or until cheese is melted and tortillas are lightly browned. Cut into quarters; top each tortilla wedge with 1 tablespoon salsa and 1 teaspoon sour cream. Transfer to serving plate. Garnish with chopped fresh cilantro, if desired.

Nutrients per Serving:
Calories: 105 (30% of calories from fat), Carbohydrate: 13g, Total Fat: 4g, Protein: 7g, Cholesterol: 8mg, Sodium: 259mg, Fiber: 1g

Mushrooms Rockefeller

Makes 18 appetizers

18 large fresh button mushrooms (about 1 pound)
 2 slices bacon
¼ cup chopped onion
 1 package (10 ounces) frozen chopped spinach, thawed and squeezed dry
 1 tablespoon lemon juice
 1 teaspoon grated lemon peel
½ jar (2 ounces) chopped pimientoes, drained
    Lemon slices and lemon balm for garnish

1. Lightly spray 13×9-inch baking dish with nonstick cooking spray. Preheat oven to 375°F. Brush dirt from mushrooms; clean by wiping mushrooms with damp paper towel. Pull entire stem out of each mushroom cap.

2. Cut thin slice from base of each stem; discard. Chop stems.

3. Cook bacon in medium skillet over medium heat until crisp. Remove bacon with tongs to paper towel; set aside. Add mushroom stems and onion to hot drippings in skillet. Cook and stir until onion is soft. Add spinach, lemon juice, lemon peel and pimientoes; blend well. Stuff mushroom caps with spinach mixture; place in single layer in prepared baking dish. Crumble reserved bacon and sprinkle on top of mushrooms. Bake 15 minutes or until heated through. Garnish, if desired. Serve immediately.

Nutrients per Serving:
Calories: 17 (35% of calories from fat), Carbohydrate: 2g, Total Fat: <1g, Protein: 2g, Cholesterol: <1mg, Sodium: 26mg, Fiber: 1g

Roasted Garlic Spread with Three Cheeses
Makes 21 servings

2 medium heads garlic
2 packages (8 ounces each) fat-free cream cheese, softened
1 package (3½ ounces) goat cheese
2 tablespoons (1 ounce) crumbled blue cheese
1 teaspoon dried thyme leaves
  Yellow bell pepper wedges, cucumber slices, carrot slices and whole radishes

1. Preheat oven to 400°F. Cut tops off garlic heads to expose tops of cloves. Place garlic in small baking pan; bake 45 minutes or until garlic is very tender. Remove from pan; cool completely. Squeeze garlic into small bowl; mash with fork.

2. Beat cream cheese and goat cheese in small bowl until smooth; stir in blue cheese, garlic and thyme. Cover; refrigerate 3 hours or overnight. Spoon dip into serving bowl; serve with yellow bell peppers, cucumbers, carrots, and radishes. Garnish with fresh thyme and red bell pepper strip, if desired.

Nutrients per Serving:
Calories: 37 (29% of calories from fat), Carbohydrate: 2g, Total Fat: 1g, Protein: 4g, Cholesterol: 9mg, Sodium: 157mg, Fiber: <1g

Food Fact

When buying garlic, choose firm, dry heads with tightly closed cloves and smooth skin. Avoid garlic with sprouting green shoots. Store, unwrapped, in a cool, dry, dark place with good ventilation for 2 to 3 months.

Angelic Deviled Eggs

Makes 12 servings

6 eggs
¼ cup low-fat (1%) cottage cheese
3 tablespoons prepared fat-free ranch dressing
2 teaspoons Dijon mustard
2 tablespoons minced fresh chives or dill
1 tablespoon diced well-drained pimiento or roasted red pepper

1. Place eggs in medium saucepan; add enough water to cover. Bring to a boil over medium heat. Remove from heat; cover. Let stand 15 minutes. Drain. Add cold water to eggs in saucepan; let stand until eggs are cool. Drain. Remove shells from eggs; discard shells.

2. Cut eggs lengthwise in half. Remove yolks, reserving 3 yolk halves. Discard remaining yolks or reserve for another use. Place egg whites, cut sides up, on serving plate; cover with plastic wrap. Refrigerate while preparing filling.

3. Combine cottage cheese, dressing, mustard and reserved yolk halves in food processor; process until smooth. (Or, place in small bowl and mash with fork until well blended.) Transfer cheese mixture to small bowl; stir in chives and pimiento. Spoon into egg whites. Cover and chill at least 1 hour. Garnish, if desired.

Nutrients per Serving:
Calories: 24 (26% of calories from fat), Carbohydrate: 1g, Total Fat: 1g, Protein: 3g, Cholesterol: 27mg, Sodium: 96mg, Fiber: 1g

Buffalo Chicken Tenders

Makes 10 servings

 3 tablespoons Louisiana-style hot sauce
½ teaspoon paprika
¼ teaspoon ground red pepper
 1 pound chicken tenders
½ cup fat-free blue cheese dressing
¼ cup reduced-fat sour cream
 2 tablespoons crumbled blue cheese
 1 medium red bell pepper, cut into ½-inch slices

1. Preheat oven to 375°F. Combine hot sauce, paprika and ground red pepper in small bowl; brush on all surfaces of chicken. Place chicken in greased 11×7-inch baking dish. Cover; marinate in refrigerator 30 minutes.

2. Bake, uncovered, about 15 minutes or until chicken is no longer pink in center.

3. Combine blue cheese dressing, sour cream and blue cheese in small serving bowl. Garnish as desired. Serve with chicken and bell pepper slices for dipping.

Nutrients per Serving:
Calories: 83 (27% of calories from fat), Carbohydrate: 5g, Total Fat: 2g, Protein: 9g, Cholesterol: 27mg, Sodium: 180mg, Fiber: 0g

Carpaccio di Zucchini

Makes 4 servings

¾ **pound zucchini, shredded**
½ **cup sliced almonds, toasted**
1 **tablespoon prepared Italian dressing**
4 **French bread baguettes, sliced in half lengthwise**
4 **teaspoons soft spread margarine**
3 **tablespoons grated Parmesan cheese**
  Halved cherry tomatoes (optional)

1. Preheat broiler. Place zucchini in medium bowl. Add almonds and dressing; mix well. Set aside.

2. Place baguette halves on large baking sheet; spread evenly with margarine. Sprinkle with cheese. Broil 3 inches from heat 2 to 3 minutes or until edges and cheese are browned.

3. Spread zucchini mixture evenly on each baguette half. Top with tomatoes, if desired. Serve immediately.

Nutrients per Serving:
Calories: 180 (75% calories from fat), Carbohydrate: 6g, Total Fat: 15g, Protein: 6g, Cholesterol: 4mg, Sodium: 305mg, Fiber: 2g

Food Fact

To toast almonds, spread in single layer on baking sheet. Bake in preheated 350°F oven 8 to 10 minutes or until golden brown, stirring frequently.

28

Spicy Orange Chicken Kabob Appetizers

Makes 12 servings

> 2 boneless skinless chicken breasts (about 8 ounces)
> 1 small red or green bell pepper
> 24 small fresh button mushrooms
> ½ cup orange juice
> 2 tablespoons reduced-sodium soy sauce
> 1 tablespoon vegetable oil
> 1½ teaspoons onion powder
> ½ teaspoon Chinese five-spice powder

1. Cut chicken and pepper each into 24 (¾-inch) square pieces. Place chicken, pepper and mushrooms in large resealable plastic food storage bag. Combine orange juice, soy sauce, oil, onion powder and five-spice powder in small bowl. Pour over chicken mixture. Close bag securely; turn to coat. Marinate in refrigerator 4 to 24 hours, turning frequently.

2. Soak 24 small wooden skewers or toothpicks in water 20 minutes. Meanwhile, preheat broiler. Coat broiler pan with nonstick cooking spray.

3. Drain chicken, pepper and mushrooms, reserving marinade. Thread 1 piece chicken, 1 piece pepper and 1 mushroom onto each skewer. Place on prepared pan. Brush with marinade; discard remaining marinade. Broil 4 inches from heat source 5 to 6 minutes or until chicken is no longer pink in center. Serve immediately.

Nutrients per Serving:
Calories: 30 (26% of calories from fat), Carbohydrate: 2g, Total Fat: <1g, Protein: 4g, Cholesterol: 10mg, Sodium: 38mg, Fiber: <1g

Crab Cakes Canton

Makes 6 servings (12 cakes)

      7 ounces thawed frozen cooked crabmeat or imitation crabmeat, drained and flaked
 1½ cups fresh whole wheat bread crumbs (about 3 bread slices)
      ¼ cup thinly sliced green onions
      1 clove garlic, minced
      1 teaspoon minced fresh ginger
      2 egg whites, lightly beaten
      1 tablespoon teriyaki sauce
      2 teaspoons vegetable oil, divided
        Prepared sweet-and-sour sauce (optional)

1. Combine crabmeat, bread crumbs, onions, garlic and ginger in medium bowl; mix well. Add egg whites and teriyaki sauce; mix well. Shape into patties about ½ inch thick and 2 inches in diameter.*

2. Heat 1 teaspoon oil in large nonstick skillet over medium heat until hot. Add about half of crab cakes to skillet. Cook 2 minutes per side or until golden brown. Remove to warm serving plate; keep warm. Repeat with remaining 1 teaspoon oil and crab cakes. Serve with sweet-and-sour sauce, if desired.

Crab cakes may be made ahead to this point; cover and refrigerate up to 24 hours before cooking.

Nutrients per Serving:
Calories: 84 (27% of calories from fat), Carbohydrate: 6g, Total Fat: 2g, Protein: 9g, Cholesterol: 18mg, Sodium: 480mg, Fiber: <1g

Ham and Cheese "Sushi" Rolls

Makes 8 servings

4 thin slices deli ham (about 4×4 inches)
1 package (8 ounces) cream cheese, softened
1 seedless cucumber, quartered lengthwise and cut into 4-inch lengths
4 thin slices (about 4×4 inches) American or Cheddar cheese, at room temperature
1 red bell pepper, cut into thin 4-inch-long strips

1. For ham sushi: Pat each ham slice with paper towel to remove excess moisture. Spread each ham slice to edges with 2 tablespoons cream cheese.

2. Pat 1 cucumber quarter with paper towel to remove excess moisture; place at edge of ham slice. Roll tightly. Seal by pressing gently. Roll in plastic wrap; refrigerate. Repeat with remaining three ham slices.

3. For cheese sushi: Spread each cheese slice to edges with 2 tablespoons cream cheese.

4. Place 2 strips red pepper even with one edge of one cheese slice. Roll tightly. Seal by pressing gently. Roll in plastic wrap; refrigerate. Repeat with remaining 3 cheese slices.

5. To serve: Remove plastic wrap from ham and cheese rolls. Cut each roll into 8 (½-inch-wide) pieces. Arrange on plate.

Nutrients per Serving:
Calories: 145 (81% of calories from fat), Carbohydrate: 3g, Total Fat: 13g, Protein: 5g, Cholesterol: 40mg, Sodium: 263mg, Fiber: <1g

Jerk Wings with Ranch Dipping Sauce

Makes 6 to 7 servings

½ cup mayonnaise
½ cup plain yogurt or sour cream
1½ teaspoons salt, divided
1¼ teaspoons garlic powder, divided
½ teaspoon black pepper, divided
¼ teaspoon onion powder
2 tablespoons orange juice
1 teaspoon sugar
1 teaspoon dried thyme leaves
1 teaspoon paprika
¼ teaspoon ground nutmeg
¼ teaspoon ground red pepper
2½ pounds chicken wings (about 10 wings)

1. Preheat oven to 450°F. For Ranch Dipping Sauce, combine mayonnaise, yogurt, ½ teaspoon salt, ¼ teaspoon garlic powder, ¼ teaspoon black pepper and onion powder in small bowl.

2. Combine orange juice, sugar, thyme, paprika, nutmeg, red pepper, remaining 1 teaspoon salt, 1 teaspoon garlic powder and ¼ teaspoon black pepper in small bowl.

3. Cut tips from wings; discard. Place wings in large bowl. Drizzle with orange juice mixture; toss to coat.

4. Transfer chicken to greased broiler pan. Bake 25 to 30 minutes or until juices run clear and skin is crisp. Serve with Ranch Dipping Sauce.

Serving Suggestion: Serve with celery sticks.

Nutrients per Serving:
Calories: 363 (50% of calories from fat), Carbohydrate: 4g, Total Fat: 30g, Protein: 20g, Cholesterol: 69mg, Sodium: 699mg, Fiber: <1g

Smoked Salmon Appetizers

Makes about 2 dozen appetizers

¼ **cup reduced-fat or fat-free cream cheese, softened**
1 **tablespoon chopped fresh dill** *or* **1 teaspoon dried dill weed**
⅛ **teaspoon ground red pepper**
4 **ounces thinly sliced smoked salmon or lox**
24 **melba toast rounds or other low-fat crackers**

1. Combine cream cheese, dill and pepper in small bowl; stir to blend. Spread evenly over each slice of salmon. Roll up salmon slices jelly-roll fashion. Place on plate; cover with plastic wrap. Chill at least 1 hour or up to 4 hours before serving.

2. Using sharp knife, cut salmon rolls crosswise into ¾-inch pieces. Place pieces, cut side down, on melba rounds. Garnish each salmon roll with dill sprig, if desired. Serve cold or at room temperature.

Nutrients per Serving:
Calories: 80 (21% of calories from fat), Carbohydrate: 10g, Total Fat: 2g, Protein: 6g, Cholesterol: 6mg, Sodium: 241mg, Fiber: 1g

Food Fact

Fresh herbs are very perishable, so purchase them in small amounts. For short-term storage, place the herb stems in water. Cover leaves loosely with a plastic bag or plastic wrap and store in the refrigerator. They will last from two days (basil, chives, dill, mint, oregano) to five days (rosemary, sage, tarragon, thyme).

Cheddar Cheese and Rice Roll

Makes 15 servings

2 cups cooked UNCLE BEN'S® ORIGINAL CONVERTED® Brand Rice
3 cups grated low-fat Cheddar cheese
¾ cup fat-free cream cheese, softened
1 can (4½ ounces) green chilies, drained, chopped
⅛ teaspoon hot sauce
1½ cups chopped walnuts

PREP: CLEAN: Wash hands. Combine rice, Cheddar cheese, cream cheese, chilies and hot sauce. Mix by hand or in food processor. Shape mixture into a log. Roll in walnuts. Wrap tightly with plastic wrap and refrigerate 1 hour.

SERVE: Serve with assorted crackers.

CHILL: Refrigerate leftovers immediately.

Nutrients per Serving:
Calories: 168 (52% of calories from fat), Carbohydrate: 10g, Total Fat: 10g, Protein: 11g, Cholesterol: 7mg, Sodium: 260mg, Fiber: 1g

Herbed-Stuffed Tomatoes

Makes 5 servings

15 cherry tomatoes
½ cup low-fat (1%) cottage cheese
1 tablespoon thinly sliced green onion
1 teaspoon chopped fresh chervil *or* ¼ teaspoon dried chervil leaves
½ teaspoon snipped fresh dill *or* ⅛ teaspoon dried dill weed
⅛ teaspoon lemon pepper

Cut thin slice off bottom of each tomato. Scoop out pulp with small spoon; discard pulp. Invert tomatoes onto paper towels to drain. Combine cottage cheese, green onion, chervil, dill and lemon pepper in small bowl. Spoon into tomatoes. Serve at once, or cover and refrigerate up to 8 hours.

Nutrients per Serving:
Calories: 27 (12% of calories from fat), Carbohydrate: 3g, Total Fat: <1g, Protein: 3g, Cholesterol: 1mg, Sodium: 96mg, Fiber: <1g

Broiled SPAM™ Appetizers

Makes 32 appetizers

1 (7-ounce) can SPAM® Classic, finely cubed
⅓ cup shredded Cheddar cheese
¼ cup finely chopped celery
¼ cup mayonnaise or salad dressing
1 tablespoon chopped fresh parsley
⅛ teaspoon hot pepper sauce
    Toast triangles, party rye slices or crackers

In medium bowl, combine all ingredients except toast. Spread mixture on toast triangles. Place on baking sheet. Broil 1 to 2 minutes or until cheese is melted.

Nutrients per Serving:
Calories: 36 (87% of calories from fat), Carbohydrate: <1g, Total Fat: 3g, Protein: 1g, Cholesterol: 6mg, Sodium: 100mg, Fiber: <1g

Herbed Stuffed Tomatoes

Spicy Shrimp Cocktail

Makes 6 servings

2 tablespoons olive or vegetable oil
¼ cup finely chopped onion
1 tablespoon chopped green bell pepper
1 clove garlic, minced
1 can (8 ounces) CONTADINA® Tomato Sauce
1 tablespoon chopped pitted green olives, drained
¼ teaspoon red pepper flakes
1 pound cooked shrimp, chilled

1. Heat oil in small skillet. Add onion, bell pepper and garlic; sauté until vegetables are tender. Stir in tomato sauce, olives and red pepper flakes.

2. Bring to a boil; simmer, uncovered, for 5 minutes. Cover. Remove from heat.

3. Chill thoroughly. Combine sauce with shrimp in small bowl.

Note: Serve over mixed greens, if desired.

Prep Time: 6 minutes
Cook Time: 10 minutes

Nutrients per Serving:
Calories: 129 (39% of calories from fat), Carbohydrate: 3g, Total Fat: 6g, Protein: 17g, Cholesterol: 147mg, Sodium: 402mg, Fiber: 1g

Turkey-Broccoli Roll-Ups

Makes 20 servings

2 pounds broccoli spears
⅓ cup fat-free sour cream
¼ cup reduced-fat mayonnaise
2 tablespoons thawed frozen orange juice concentrate
1 tablespoon Dijon mustard
1 teaspoon dried basil leaves
1 pound smoked turkey, very thinly sliced

1. Arrange broccoli spears in single layer in large, shallow microwavable dish. Add 1 tablespoon water. Cover dish tightly with plastic wrap; vent. Microwave at HIGH (100%) 6 to 7 minutes or just until broccoli is crisp-tender, rearranging spears after 4 minutes. Carefully remove plastic wrap; drain broccoli. Immediately place broccoli in cold water to stop cooking; drain well. Pat dry with paper towels.

2. Combine sour cream, mayonnaise, juice concentrate, mustard and basil in small bowl; mix well.

3. Cut turkey slices into 2-inch-wide strips. Spread sour cream mixture evenly on strips. Place 1 broccoli piece at short end of each strip. Starting at short end, roll up tightly (allow broccoli spear to protrude from one end). Place on serving platter; cover with plastic wrap. Refrigerate until ready to serve. Garnish just before serving, if desired.

Note: To blanch broccoli on stove top, bring small amount of water to a boil in saucepan. Add broccoli spears; cover. Simmer 2 to 3 minutes or until broccoli is crisp-tender; drain. Cool; continue as directed.

Nutrients per Serving:
Calories: 51 (19% of calories from fat), Carbohydrate: 4g, Total Fat: 1g, Protein: 7g, Cholesterol: 10mg, Sodium: 259mg, Fiber: 2g

Far East Tabbouleh

Makes 4 servings

¾ cup uncooked bulgur
1¾ cups boiling water
2 tablespoons reduced-sodium teriyaki sauce
2 tablespoons lemon juice
1 tablespoon olive oil
¾ cup diced seeded cucumber
¾ cup diced seeded tomato
½ cup thinly sliced green onions
½ cup minced fresh cilantro or parsley
1 tablespoon minced fresh ginger
1 clove garlic, minced

1. Combine bulgur and water in small bowl. Cover with plastic wrap; let stand 45 minutes or until bulgur is puffed, stirring occasionally. Drain in wire mesh sieve; discard liquid.

2. Combine bulgur, teriyaki sauce, lemon juice and oil in large bowl. Stir in cucumber, tomato, onions, cilantro, ginger and garlic until well blended. Cover; refrigerate 4 hours, stirring occasionally. Garnish as desired.

Nutrients per Serving:
Calories: 73 (23% of calories from fat), Carbohydrate: 13g, Total Fat: 2g, Protein: 2g, Cholesterol: 0mg, Sodium: 156mg, Fiber: 3g

Confetti Tuna in Celery Sticks

Makes 10 to 12 servings

1 (3-ounce) pouch of STARKIST® Premium Albacore or Chunk Light Tuna
½ cup shredded red or green cabbage
½ cup shredded carrot
¼ cup shredded yellow squash or zucchini
3 tablespoons reduced-calorie cream cheese, softened
1 tablespoon plain low-fat yogurt
½ teaspoon dried basil, crushed
　 Salt and pepper to taste
10 to 12 (4-inch) celery sticks, with leaves if desired

1. In a small bowl toss together tuna, cabbage, carrot and squash.

2. Stir in cream cheese, yogurt and basil. Add salt and pepper to taste.

3. With small spatula spread mixture evenly into celery sticks.

Nutrients per Serving:
Calories: 32 (26% of calories from fat), Carbohydrate: 3g, Total Fat: 1g, Protein: 3g,
Cholesterol: 5mg, Sodium: 90mg, Fiber: 1g

Seafood Spread

Makes 1½ cups (12 servings)

  1 **package (8 ounces) cream cheese, softened**
½ **pound smoked whitefish, skinned, boned and flaked**
  2 **tablespoons minced green onion**
  1 **tablespoon plus 1 teaspoon chopped fresh dill**
  1 **teaspoon lemon juice**
¼ **teaspoon black pepper**

Beat cream cheese in medium bowl at medium speed of electric mixer until smooth. Add remaining ingredients except bread, mixing until blended. Refrigerate until ready to serve. Serve with rye bread slices or assorted crackers. Garnish with lime wedges, if desired.

Nutrients per Serving:
Calories: 87 (70% of calories from fat), Carbohydrate: 1g, Total Fat: 7g, Protein: 6g, Cholesterol: 27mg, Sodium: 249mg, Fiber: <1g

Cheesy Chips

Makes 4 servings

10 **wonton wrappers**
 2 **tablespoons powdered American cheese or grated Parmesan cheese**
 2 **teaspoons olive oil**
⅛ **teaspoon garlic powder**

Preheat oven to 375°F. Spray baking sheet with nonstick cooking spray. Diagonally cut each wonton wrapper in half, forming two triangles. Place in single layer on prepared baking sheet. Combine cheese, oil and garlic powder in small bowl. Sprinkle over wonton triangles. Bake 6 to 8 minutes or until golden brown and crisp. Remove from oven. Cool completely.

Nutrients per Serving:
Calories: 75 (38% of calories from fat), Carbohydrate: 9g, Total Fat: 3g, Protein: 2g, Cholesterol: 4mg, Sodium: 92mg, Fiber: <1g

Jicama & Shrimp Cocktail with Roasted Red Pepper Sauce

Makes 8 servings

- 2 large red bell peppers
- 6 ounces (about 24 medium-large) shrimp, peeled and deveined
- 1 medium clove garlic
- 1½ cups fresh cilantro sprigs
- 2 tablespoons lime juice
- 2 tablespoons orange juice
- ½ teaspoon hot pepper sauce
- 1 small jicama (about ¾ pound), peeled and cut into strips
- 1 plum tomato, halved, seeded and thinly sliced

1. Place bell peppers on broiler pan. Broil, 4 to 6 inches from heat, about 6 minutes, turning every 2 to 3 minutes or until all sides are charred. Transfer peppers to paper bag; close bag tightly. Let stand 10 minutes or until peppers are cool enough to handle and skins are loosened. Peel peppers; cut in half. Remove cores, seeds and membranes; discard.

2. Add shrimp to large saucepan of boiling water. Reduce heat to medium-low; simmer, uncovered, 2 to 3 minutes or until shrimp turn pink. Drain shrimp; rinse under cold running water. Cover; refrigerate until ready to use.

3. Place peppers and garlic in food processor; process until peppers are coarsely chopped. Add cilantro, lime juice, orange juice and pepper sauce; process until cilantro is finely chopped but mixture is not puréed.

4. Combine jicama, shrimp and tomato in large bowl. Add bell pepper mixture; toss to coat evenly. Serve over lettuce.

Nutrients per Serving:
Calories: 69 (7% of calories from fat), Carbohydrate: 10g, Total Fat: 1g, Protein: 6g, Cholesterol: 42mg, Sodium: 120mg, Fiber: 1g

Hummus-Stuffed Vegetables

Makes 12 servings

  1 can (15 ounces) chick-peas, rinsed and drained
  1 tablespoon lemon juice
  1 tablespoon olive oil
  1 medium clove garlic
  ½ teaspoon ground cumin
  ¼ teaspoon salt
  ¼ teaspoon black pepper
  1 cup Chinese pea pods (about 24)
  ¾ pound medium fresh mushrooms (about 24)

1. Combine chick-peas, lemon juice, oil, garlic, cumin, salt and pepper in food processor. Process until smooth. Transfer to pastry bag fitted with fluted tip.

2. Remove strings from pea pods. (Some pea pods will not have a stringy portion.) Carefully split pea pods with tip of paring knife. Remove stems from mushrooms; discard.

3. Pipe bean mixture into pea pods and into mushroom caps. Store loosely covered in refrigerator until ready to serve. Garnish just before serving, if desired.

Variation: Substitute cucumber slices or red or green bell peppers, cut into 1½-inch triangles, for pea pods and mushrooms.

Nutrients per Serving:
Calories: 56 (29% of calories from fat), Carbohydrate: 8g, Total Fat: 2g, Protein: 3g, Cholesterol: 0mg, Sodium: 187mg, Fiber: 2g

Beef

Oriental Flank Steak

Makes about 4 servings

   ¾ **cup WISH-BONE® Italian Dressing***
   3 **tablespoons soy sauce**
   3 **tablespoons firmly packed brown sugar**
   ½ **teaspoon ground ginger (optional)**
   1 **to 1½ pounds flank, top round or sirloin steak**

*Also terrific with Wish-Bone® Robusto Italian, Lite Italian or Red Wine Vinaigrette Dressing.

In small bowl, combine all ingredients except steak.

In large, shallow nonaluminum baking dish or plastic bag, pour ½ cup marinade over steak. Cover, or close bag, and marinate in refrigerator, turning occasionally, 3 to 24 hours. Refrigerate remaining marinade.

Remove steak from marinade, discarding marinade. Grill or broil steak, turning once and brushing frequently with reserved marinade, until steak is desired doneness.

Nutrients per Serving:
Calories: 272 (49% of calories from fat), Carbohydrate: 9g, Total Fat: 15g, Protein: 25g, Cholesterol: 46mg, Sodium: 888mg, Fiber: <1g

Beef Bourguignon

Makes 10 to 12 servings

         1 to 2 boneless beef top sirloin steaks (about 3 pounds)
        ½ cup all-purpose flour
         4 slices bacon, diced
         8 small new red potatoes, unpeeled, cut into quarters
         8 to 10 mushrooms, sliced
         2 medium carrots, diced
        20 to 24 pearl onions
         3 cloves garlic, minced
         1 bay leaf
         1 teaspoon dried marjoram leaves
        ½ teaspoon dried thyme leaves
        ½ teaspoon salt
           Black pepper
        2½ cups Burgundy wine or beef broth

Slow Cooker Directions

1. Cut beef into ½-inch pieces. Coat with flour, shaking off excess; set aside.

2. Cook bacon in large skillet over medium heat until partially cooked. Add beef; cook until browned. Remove beef and bacon with slotted spoon.

3. Layer potatoes, mushrooms, carrots, onions, garlic, bay leaf, marjoram, thyme, salt, pepper to taste, beef and bacon mixture in slow cooker. Pour wine over all. Cover; cook on LOW 8 to 9 hours or until beef is tender. Remove and discard bay leaf before serving.

Nutrients per Serving:
Calories: 268 (23% of calories from fat), Carbohydrate: 14g, Total Fat: 7g, Protein: 26g, Cholesterol: 73mg, Sodium: 287mg, Fiber: 1g

Beef & Blue Cheese Salad

Makes 4 main-dish or 8 side-dish servings

1 package (10 ounces) mixed green lettuce leaves
4 ounces sliced rare deli roast beef, cut into thin strips
1 large tomato, seeded and coarsely chopped *or* 8 large cherry tomatoes, halved
1 cup croutons
2 ounces (½ cup) crumbed blue or Gorgonzola cheese
½ cup prepared Caesar or Italian salad dressing

1. In large bowl, combine lettuce, roast beef, tomato, croutons and cheese.

2. Drizzle with dressing; toss well. Serve immediately.

Nutrients per Serving:
Calories: 288 (70% of calories from fat), Carbohydrate: 11g, Total Fat: 23g, Protein: 11g,
Cholesterol: 21mg, Sodium: 872mg, Fiber: 2g

Food Fact

Gorgonzola is one of Italy's great cheeses. It has an ivory-colored interior that is streaked with bluish-green veins, is made from cow's milk and has a creamy savory flavor. It can be found cut into wedges and wrapped in foil in most supermarkets.

Main-Dish Pie

Makes 6 servings

1 package (8 rolls) refrigerated crescent rolls
1 pound lean ground beef
1 medium onion, chopped
1 can (12 ounces) beef or mushroom gravy
1 box (10 ounces) BIRDS EYE® frozen Green Peas, thawed
½ cup shredded Swiss cheese
6 slices tomato

• Preheat oven to 350°F.

• Unroll dough and separate rolls. Spread to cover bottom of ungreased 9-inch pie pan. Press together to form lower crust. Bake 10 minutes.

• Meanwhile, in large skillet, brown ground beef and onion; drain excess fat.

• Stir in gravy and peas; cook until heated through.

• Pour mixture into partially baked crust. Sprinkle with cheese.

• Bake 10 to 15 minutes or until crust is brown and cheese is melted.

• Arrange tomato slices over pie; bake 2 minutes more.

Nutrients per Serving:
Calories: 345 (48% of calories from fat), Carbohydrate: 15g, Total Fat: 18g, Protein: 29g, Cholesterol: 84mg, Sodium: 529mg, Fiber: 4g

Japanese-Style Steak with Garden Sunomono

Makes 4 servings

Garden Sunomono

  1 medium cucumber, peeled, seeded and thinly sliced
½ teaspoon salt
¼ cup rice wine vinegar
  3 tablespoons sugar
  1 cup thinly sliced radishes
½ cup matchstick-size carrot strips

Japanese-Style Steak

  3 New York strip steaks, cut ¾-inch thick (8 ounces each)
¼ cup soy sauce
  3 tablespoons dry sherry
  1 teaspoon dark sesame oil
½ teaspoon ground ginger
  1 large clove garlic, minced

1. For sunomono, place cucumber in colander; sprinkle with salt. Let stand 20 minutes. Squeeze out liquid; rinse with water. Squeeze again.

2. Combine vinegar and sugar in medium bowl; stir until sugar dissolves. Add cucumber, radishes and carrot. Cover; refrigerate 30 minutes to 2 hours, stirring occasionally.

3. Place steaks in shallow baking dish. Blend soy sauce, sherry, oil, ginger and garlic in small bowl; pour over steaks. Cover; refrigerate 30 minutes to 2 hours, turning steaks occasionally.

4. To complete recipe, preheat broiler. Remove steaks from marinade; place on broiler pan rack. Discard marinade. Broil 2 to 3 inches from heat 5 to 6 minutes per side or until desired doneness.

5. Transfer steaks to cutting board; slice across the grain into ½-inch slices. Serve with sunomono.

Nutrients per Serving:
Calories: 348 (34% of calories from fat), Carbohydrate: 16g, Total Fat: 13g, Protein: 39g, Cholesterol: 79mg, Sodium: 701mg, Fiber: 1g

Veal in Gingered Sweet Bell Pepper Sauce

Makes 4 servings

1 teaspoon olive oil
¾ pound veal cutlets, thinly sliced
½ cup fat-free (skim) milk
1 tablespoon finely chopped fresh tarragon
2 teaspoons crushed capers
1 jar (7 ounces) roasted red peppers, drained
1 tablespoon lemon juice
½ teaspoon freshly grated ginger
½ teaspoon black pepper

1. Heat oil in medium saucepan over high heat. Add veal; lightly brown both sides. Reduce heat to medium. Add milk, chopped tarragon and capers. Cook, uncovered, 5 minutes or until veal is fork-tender and milk evaporates.

2. Place roasted peppers, lemon juice, ginger and black pepper in food processor or blender; process until smooth. Set aside.

3. Remove veal from pan with slotted spoon; place in serving dish. Spoon roasted pepper sauce over veal. Sprinkle with cooked capers and fresh tarragon, if desired.

Nutrients per Serving:
Calories: 120 (31% of calories from fat), Carbohydrate: 6g, Total Fat: 4g, Protein: 14g, Cholesterol: 54mg, Sodium: 89mg, Fiber: 1g

Braciola

Makes 8 servings

1 can (28 ounces) tomato sauce
2½ teaspoons dried oregano leaves, divided
1¼ teaspoons dried basil leaves, divided
1 teaspoon salt
½ pound bulk hot Italian sausage
½ cup chopped onion
¼ cup grated Parmesan cheese
2 cloves garlic, minced
1 tablespoon dried parsley flakes
1 to 2 beef flank steaks (about 2½ pounds)

Slow Cooker Directions

1. Combine tomato sauce, 2 teaspoons oregano, 1 teaspoon basil and salt in medium bowl; set aside.

2. Cook sausage in large nonstick skillet over medium-high heat until no longer pink stirring to separate; drain well. Combine sausage, onion, cheese, garlic, parsley, remaining ½ teaspoon oregano and ¼ teaspoon basil in medium bowl; set aside.

3. Place steak on countertop between two pieces waxed paper. Pound with meat mallet until steak is ⅛ to ¼ inch thick. Cut steak into about 3-inch wide strips.

4. Spoon sausage mixture evenly onto each steak strip. Roll up, jelly-roll style, securing meat with toothpicks. Place each roll in slow cooker. Pour reserved tomato sauce mixture over meat. Cover; cook on LOW 6 to 8 hours.

5. Cut each roll into slices. Arrange slices on dinner plates. Top with hot tomato sauce.

Nutrients per Serving:
Calories: 349 (44% of calories from fat), Carbohydrate: 9g, Total Fat: 17g, Protein: 38g, Cholesterol: 78mg, Sodium: 1182mg, Fiber: 2g

Joe's Special
Makes 4 to 6 servings

Nonstick cooking spray
1 pound lean ground beef
2 cups sliced mushrooms
1 small onion, chopped
2 teaspoons Worcestershire sauce
1 teaspoon dried oregano leaves
1 teaspoon ground nutmeg
½ teaspoon garlic powder
½ teaspoon salt
1 package (10 ounces) frozen chopped spinach, thawed
4 large eggs, lightly beaten
⅓ cup grated Parmesan cheese

1. Spray large skillet with cooking spray. Add ground beef, mushrooms and onion; cook over medium-high heat 6 to 8 minutes or until onion is tender, breaking beef apart with wooden spoon. Add Worcestershire, oregano, nutmeg, garlic powder and salt. Cook until meat is no longer pink.

2. Drain spinach (do not squeeze dry); stir into meat mixture. Push mixture to one side of pan. Reduce heat to medium. Pour eggs into other side of pan; cook, without stirring, 1 to 2 minutes or until set on bottom. Lift eggs to allow uncooked portion to flow underneath. Repeat until softly set. Gently stir into meat mixture and heat through. Stir in cheese.

Nutrients per Serving:
Calories: 369 (56% of calories from fat), Carbohydrate: 8g, Total Fat: 23g, Protein: 32g, Cholesterol: 290mg, Sodium: 614mg, Fiber: 1g

Sirloin with Sweet Caramelized Onions

Makes 4 servings

Nonstick cooking spray
1 medium onion, very thinly sliced
1 boneless beef top sirloin steak (about 1 pound)
¼ cup water
2 tablespoons Worcestershire sauce
1 tablespoon sugar

1. Lightly coat 12-inch skillet with cooking spray; heat over high heat until hot. Add onion; cook and stir 4 minutes or until browned. Remove from skillet and set aside. Wipe out skillet with paper towel.

2. Coat same skillet with cooking spray; heat until hot. Add beef; cook 10 to 13 minutes for medium-rare to medium, turning once. Remove from heat and transfer to cutting board; let stand 3 minutes before slicing.

3. Meanwhile, return skillet to high heat until hot; add onion, water, Worcestershire sauce and sugar. Cook 30 to 45 seconds or until most liquid has evaporated.

4. Thinly slice beef on the diagonal and serve with onions.

Nutrients per Serving:
Calories: 159 (28% of calories from fat), Carbohydrate: 7g, Total Fat: 5g, Protein: 21g, Cholesterol: 60mg, Sodium: 118mg, Fiber: 1g

Beefy Bean & Walnut Stir-Fry

Makes 4 servings

1 teaspoon vegetable oil
3 cloves garlic, minced
1 pound lean ground beef or ground turkey
1 bag (16 ounces) BIRDS EYE® frozen Cut Green Beans, thawed
1 teaspoon salt
½ cup walnut pieces

• In large skillet, heat oil and garlic over medium heat about 30 seconds.

• Add beef and beans; sprinkle with salt. Mix well.

• Cook 5 minutes or until beef is well browned, stirring occasionally.

• Stir in walnuts; cook 2 minutes more.

Birds Eye® Idea: When you add California walnuts to Birds Eye® vegetables, you not only add texture and a great nutty taste, but nutrition too.

Nutrients per Serving:
Calories: 467 (63% of calories from fat), Carbohydrate: 11g, Total Fat: 33g, Protein: 32g, Cholesterol: 88mg, Sodium: 645mg, Fiber: 4g

Peppercorn Steaks

Makes 4 servings

2 tablespoons olive oil
1 to 2 teaspoons cracked red or black peppercorns or freshly ground pepper
1 teaspoon minced garlic
1 teaspoon dried herbs, such as rosemary or parsley
4 boneless beef top loin (strip) or ribeye steaks (6 ounces each)
¼ teaspoon salt

1. Combine oil, peppercorns, garlic and herbs in small bowl. Rub mixture on both sides of each steak. Cover and refrigerate.

2. Prepare grill for direct cooking.

3. Place steaks on grid over medium heat. Grill, uncovered, 10 to 12 minutes for medium-rare to medium or to desired doneness, turning occasionally. Season with salt after cooking.

Nutrients per Serving:
Calories: 413 (50% of calories from fat), Carbohydrate: <1g, Total Fat: 23g, Protein: 49g, Cholesterol: 129mg, Sodium: 249mg, Fiber: <1g

Food Fact

When purchasing dried herbs or spices, mark each container with the purchase date and discard any remaining after six months. Buy small quantities of infrequently used herbs and spices. Store in a cool, dry place in tightly covered lightproof containers. Do not place above the range as heat and moisture will cause the flavor to deteriorate more quickly.

Yankee Pot Roast and Vegetables

Makes 10 to 12 servings

1 beef chuck pot roast (2½ pounds)
  Salt and black pepper
3 medium baking potatoes (about 1 pound), unpeeled and cut into quarters
2 large carrots, cut into ¾-inch slices
2 ribs celery, cut into ¾-inch slices
1 medium onion, sliced
1 large parsnip, cut into ¾-inch slices
2 bay leaves
1 teaspoon dried rosemary
½ teaspoon dried thyme leaves
½ cup reduced-sodium beef broth

Slow Cooker Directions

1. Trim excess fat from meat and discard. Cut meat into serving pieces; sprinkle with salt and pepper.

2. Combine vegetables, bay leaves, rosemary and thyme in slow cooker. Place beef over vegetables. Pour broth over beef. Cover; cook on LOW 8½ to 9 hours or until beef is fork-tender. Remove beef to serving platter. Arrange vegetables around beef. Remove and discard bay leaves.

Cook's Nook: To make gravy, ladle the juices into a 2-cup measure; let stand 5 minutes. Skim off and discard fat. Measure remaining juices and heat to a boil in small saucepan. For each cup of juice, mix 2 tablespoons of flour with ¼ cup of cold water until smooth. Stir mixture into boiling juices, stirring constantly 1 minute or until thickened.

Nutrients per Serving:
Calories: 270 (33% of calories from fat), Carbohydrate: 15g, Total Fat: 10g, Protein: 28g, Cholesterol: 75mg, Sodium: 99mg, Fiber: 3g

Stuffed Bell Peppers

Makes 4 servings

>   1 cup chopped fresh tomatoes
>   1 teaspoon chopped fresh cilantro
>   1 jalapeño pepper,* seeded and chopped (optional)
>   ½ clove garlic, finely minced
>   ½ teaspoon dried oregano leaves, divided
>   ¼ teaspoon ground cumin
>   6 ounces lean ground beef round
>   ½ cup cooked brown rice
>   ¼ cup cholesterol-free egg substitute *or* 2 egg whites
>   2 tablespoons finely chopped onion
>   ¼ teaspoon salt
>   ⅛ teaspoon black pepper
>   2 large bell peppers, any color, seeded and cut in half lengthwise

*Jalapeño peppers can sting and irritate the skin; wear rubber gloves when handling peppers and do not touch eyes. Wash hands after handling.

1. Preheat oven to 400°F.

2. Combine tomatoes, cilantro, jalapeño pepper, if desired, garlic, ¼ teaspoon oregano and cumin in small bowl. Set aside.

3. Thoroughly combine beef, rice, egg substitute, onion, salt and black pepper in large bowl. Stir in ⅔ cup tomato mixture. Spoon filling evenly into pepper halves.

4. Spray 4 (12×12-inch) sheets heavy-duty foil with nonstick cooking spray. Place each pepper half on foil sheet. Double fold sides and ends of foil to seal packets. Place packets on baking sheet.

5. Bake 45 minutes or until meat is browned and vegetables are tender. Remove from oven. Carefully open one end of each packet to allow steam to escape. Open packets and transfer pepper halves to serving plates. Serve with remaining tomato salsa.

Nutrients per Serving:
Calories: 158 (40% of calories from fat), Carbohydrate: 13g, Total Fat: 7g, Protein: 11g, Cholesterol: 29mg, Sodium: 205mg, Fiber: 2g

Steaks with Zesty Merlot Sauce

Makes 4 servings

½ cup merlot wine
2 tablespoons Worcestershire sauce
1 tablespoon balsamic vinegar
1 teaspoon sugar
1 teaspoon beef bouillon granules
½ teaspoon dried thyme leaves
2 beef ribeye steaks (8 ounces each)
2 tablespoons finely chopped parsley

1. Combine wine, Worcestershire sauce, vinegar, sugar, bouillon granules and thyme; set aside.

2. Heat large nonstick skillet over high heat until hot. Add steaks; cook 3 minutes on each side. Turn steaks again and cook 3 to 6 minutes longer over medium heat or until desired doneness.

3. Cut steaks in half; arrange on serving platter. Place in oven to keep warm.

4. Add wine mixture to same skillet. Bring to a boil; cook and stir 1 minute, scraping up any brown bits. Spoon over steaks. Sprinkle with parsley; serve immediately.

Nutrients per Serving:
Calories: 287 (53% of calories from fat), Carbohydrate: 4g, Total Fat: 17g, Protein: 23g, Cholesterol: 58mg, Sodium: 294mg, Fiber: <1g

Food Fact

Wines of all sorts are used in cooking. Special cooking wines available in supermarkets are not recommended because they are often inferior in quality and contain salt. However, there is no need to use fine vintages for cooking. Leftover wine that is no longer good for drinking can be used in cooking. Wine can be omitted in most recipes that call for it, although adjustments in the amount of liquid may be required.

Italian-Style Meat Loaf

Makes 8 servings

  1 can (6 ounces) no-salt-added tomato paste
½ cup dry red wine plus ½ cup water *or* 1 cup water
  1 teaspoon minced garlic
½ teaspoon dried basil leaves
½ teaspoon dried oregano leaves
¼ teaspoon salt
12 ounces lean ground beef round
12 ounces ground turkey breast
  1 cup fresh whole wheat bread crumbs (2 slices whole wheat bread)
½ cup shredded zucchini
¼ cup cholesterol-free egg substitute *or* 2 egg whites

1. Preheat oven to 350°F. Combine tomato paste, wine, water, garlic, basil, oregano and salt in small saucepan. Bring to a boil; reduce heat to low. Simmer, uncovered, 15 minutes. Set aside.

2. Combine beef, turkey, bread crumbs, zucchini, egg substitute and tomato mixture, reserving ½ cup, in large bowl. Mix well. Shape into loaf; place in ungreased 9×5×3-inch loaf pan. Bake 45 minutes. Discard any drippings. Pour ½ cup remaining tomato mixture over top of loaf. Bake an additional 15 minutes. Place on serving platter. Cool 10 minutes before cutting into 8 slices. Garnish as desired.

Nutrients per Serving:
Calories: 144 (11% of calories from fat), Carbohydrate: 7g, Total Fat: 2g, Protein: 19g, Cholesterol: 41mg, Sodium: 171mg, Fiber: 1g

Grilled Beef Salad

Makes 4 servings

½ **cup mayonnaise**
2 **tablespoons cider vinegar or white wine vinegar**
1 **tablespoon spicy brown mustard**
2 **cloves garlic, minced**
½ **teaspoon sugar**
6 **cups torn assorted lettuces such as romaine, red leaf and Bibb**
1 **large tomato, seeded and chopped**
⅓ **cup chopped fresh basil**
2 **slices red onion, separated into rings**
1 **boneless beef top sirloin steak (about 1 pound)**
½ **teaspoon salt**
½ **teaspoon black pepper**
½ **cup herb or garlic croutons**
   Additional black pepper (optional)

1. Prepare grill for direct cooking. Combine mayonnaise, vinegar, mustard, garlic and sugar in small bowl; mix well. Cover and refrigerate until ready to serve.

2. Toss together lettuce, tomato, basil and onion in large bowl; cover and refrigerate until ready to serve.

3. Sprinkle both sides of steak with salt and ½ teaspoon pepper. Place steak on grid. Grill, uncovered, over medium heat 13 to 16 minutes for medium-rare to medium or until desired doneness, turning once.

4. Transfer steak to carving board. Slice in half lengthwise; carve crosswise into thin slices.

5. Add steak and croutons to bowl with lettuce mixture; toss well. Add mayonnaise mixture; toss until well coated. Serve with additional pepper, if desired.

Nutrients per Serving:
Calories: 383 (59% of calories from fat), Carbohydrate: 8g, Total Fat: 30g, Protein: 25g, Cholesterol: 75mg, Sodium: 562mg, Fiber: 2g

Salisbury Steaks with Mushroom-Wine Sauce

Makes 4 servings

1 pound lean ground beef sirloin
¾ teaspoon garlic salt or seasoned salt
¼ teaspoon black pepper
2 tablespoons butter or margarine
1 package (8 ounces) sliced button mushrooms *or* 2 packages (4 ounces each) sliced
    exotic mushrooms
2 tablespoons sweet vermouth or ruby port wine
1 jar (12 ounces) *or* 1 can (10½ ounces) beef gravy

1. Heat large heavy nonstick skillet over medium-high heat 3 minutes or until hot.* Meanwhile, combine ground sirloin, garlic salt and pepper; mix well. Shape mixture into four ¼-inch-thick oval patties.

2. Place patties in skillet as they are formed; cook 3 minutes per side or until browned. Transfer to plate. Pour off drippings.

3. Melt butter in skillet; add mushrooms. Cook and stir 2 minutes. Add vermouth; cook 1 minute. Add gravy; mix well.

4. Return patties to skillet; simmer uncovered over medium heat 2 minutes for medium or until desired doneness, turning meat and stirring sauce.

If pan is not heavy, use medium heat.

Nutrients per Serving:
Calories: 341 (61% of calories from fat), Carbohydrate: 8g, Total Fat: 23g, Protein: 24g, Cholesterol: 88mg, Sodium: 984mg, Fiber: 1g

Salisbury Steak with Mushroom-Wine Sauce

Peppercorn Beef Kabobs

Makes 4 servings

> 1 boneless beef top sirloin steak (about 1 pound)
> 1½ teaspoons black peppercorns, crushed
> 1 clove garlic, minced
> ½ teaspoon salt
> ½ teaspoon paprika
> 1 medium onion, cut into 12 wedges
>   Cherry tomato halves (optional)

1. Cut beef into 1-inch pieces. Combine peppercorns, garlic, salt and paprika in shallow dish. Add beef; toss to coat.

2. Thread an equal number of beef pieces onto each of four 12-inch skewers* along with 3 onion wedges. Place kabobs on rack in broiler pan. Broil 3 to 4 inches from heat source 9 to 12 minutes, turning occasionally. Garnish with tomatoes, if desired.

If using wooden skewers, soak in water 20 to 30 minutes before using to prevent burning.

Nutrients per Serving:
Calories: 158 (26% of calories from fat), Carbohydrate: 3g, Total Fat: 4g, Protein: 25g, Cholesterol: 54mg, Sodium: 339mg, Fiber: 1g

Food Fact

A kabob (also spelled "kebab") refers to small pieces of meat, poultry, fish and vegetables, often marinated, that are threaded onto a skewer before grilling or broiling. Examples of skewered dishes include the French brochette, the Italian spiedini, the Russian shashlik, the Middle Eastern shish kebab and the Indonesian saté. Fresh fruit kabobs are served as appetizers and desserts and may or may not be heated.

Blue Cheese-Stuffed Sirloin Patties

Makes 4 servings

1½ **pounds ground beef sirloin**
½ **cup (2 ounces) shredded sharp Cheddar cheese**
¼ **cup crumbled blue cheese**
¼ **cup finely chopped parsley**
2 **teaspoons Dijon mustard**
1 **teaspoon Worcestershire sauce**
1 **clove garlic, minced**
¼ **teaspoon salt**
2 **teaspoons olive oil**
1 **medium red bell pepper, cut into thin strips**

1. Shape beef into 8 patties about 4 inches in diameter and ¼ inch thick.

2. Combine cheeses, parsley, mustard, Worcestershire sauce, garlic and salt in small bowl; toss gently to blend.

3. Mound ¼ cheese mixture on each of 4 patties (about 3 tablespoons per patty). Top with remaining 4 patties; pinch edges of patties to seal completely. Set aside.

4. Heat oil in 12-inch nonstick skillet over medium-high heat until hot. Add pepper strips; cook and stir until edges of peppers begin to brown. Sprinkle with salt. Remove from skillet and keep warm.

5. Add beef patties to same skillet; cook on medium-high heat 5 minutes. Turn patties; top with peppers. Cook 4 minutes or until patties are no longer pink in centers (160°F).

Nutrients per Serving:
Calories: 463 (62% of calories from fat), Carbohydrate: 3g, Total Fat: 32g, Protein: 38g, Cholesterol: 131mg, Sodium: 548mg, Fiber: 1g

Blue Cheese-Stuffed Sirloin Patty

Jamaican Steak

Makes 6 servings

  2 pounds beef flank steak
  ¼ cup packed brown sugar
  3 tablespoons orange juice
  3 tablespoons lime juice
  3 cloves garlic, minced
  1 piece (1½×1 inches) fresh ginger, minced
  2 teaspoons grated orange peel
  2 teaspoons grated lime peel
  1 teaspoon salt
  1 teaspoon black pepper
  ¼ teaspoon ground cinnamon
  ⅛ teaspoon ground cloves
     Shredded orange peel
     Shredded lime peel

Score both sides of beef.* Combine sugar, juices, garlic, ginger, grated peels, salt, pepper, cinnamon and cloves in 2-quart glass dish. Add beef; turn to coat. Cover and refrigerate steak at least 2 hours. Remove beef from marinade; discard marinade. Grill beef over medium-hot KINGSFORD® Briquets about 6 minutes per side until medium-rare or to desired doneness. Garnish with shredded orange and lime peels.

*To score flank steak, cut ¼-inch-deep diagonal lines about 1 inch apart in surface of steak to form diamond-shaped design.

Nutrients per Serving:
Calories: 238 (40% of calories from fat), Carbohydrate: 1g, Total Fat: 10g, Protein: 33g, Cholesterol: 61mg, Sodium: 133mg, Fiber: <1g

Beef Pot Roast

Makes 8 servings

   1 beef eye of round roast (about 2½ pounds)
   1 can (14½ ounces) fat-free reduced-sodium beef broth
   2 cloves garlic
   1 teaspoon herbs de Provence *or* ¼ teaspoon *each* rosemary, thyme, sage and savory
   4 small turnips, peeled and cut into wedges
 10 ounces fresh brussels sprouts, trimmed
   8 ounces baby carrots
   4 ounces pearl onions, skins removed
   1 tablespoon water
   2 teaspoons cornstarch

1. Heat Dutch oven over medium-high heat. Brown roast evenly on all sides.

2. Pour broth into Dutch oven; bring to a boil over high heat. Add garlic and herbs de Provence. Cover and reduce heat; simmer 1½ hours.

3. Add turnips, brussels sprouts, carrots and onions to Dutch oven. Cover; cook 25 to 30 minutes or until vegetables are tender. Remove meat and vegetables and arrange on serving platter; cover with foil to keep warm.

4. Strain broth; return to Dutch oven. Stir water into cornstarch until smooth. Stir cornstarch mixture into broth. Bring to a boil over medium-high heat; cook and stir 1 minute or until thick and bubbly. Serve immediately with pot roast and vegetables. Garnish as desired.

Nutrients per Serving:
Calories: 261 (30% of calories from fat), Carbohydrate: 11g, Total Fat: 9g, Protein: 35g, Cholesterol: 79mg, Sodium: 142mg, Fiber: 2g

Easy Pepper Steak

Makes 4 servings

1 pound lean ground beef
1 tablespoon chopped fresh thyme *or* 1 teaspoon dried thyme leaves
1 teaspoon paprika
  Salt and black pepper
3 tablespoons all-purpose flour
1¼ cups chicken broth
2 tablespoons dry white wine
1 teaspoon Worcestershire sauce
1 *each* red, green and yellow medium bell peppers, cut into thin slices
1 medium onion, sliced, separated into rings

Microwave Directions

Crumble ground beef into large bowl. Stir in thyme, paprika, 1 teaspoon salt and dash of black pepper. Shape into four ½-inch-thick oval loaves. Place on microwave-safe rack; cover with waxed paper. Microwave at HIGH (100% power) 4 to 5 minutes or to desired doneness, turning rack after 3 minutes. Reserve ⅓ cup drippings; keep beef warm. Mix drippings and flour in medium microwave-safe bowl. Stir in broth, wine and Worcestershire sauce. Microwave at HIGH 2 to 3 minutes or until mixture thickens, stirring every minute. Season with salt and black pepper to taste. Add bell peppers and onions; cover. Microwave at HIGH 6 to 7 minutes or until vegetables are crisp-tender, stirring after 3 minutes. Serve over beef.

Nutrients per Serving:
Calories: 288 (50% of calories from fat), Carbohydrate: 13g, Total Fat: 16g, Protein: 22g, Cholesterol: 70mg, Sodium: 390mg, Fiber: 2g

London Broil with Marinated Vegetables

Makes 6 servings

¾ **cup olive oil**
¾ **cup red wine**
2 **tablespoons finely chopped shallots**
2 **tablespoons red wine vinegar**
2 **teaspoons bottled minced garlic**
½ **teaspoon dried marjoram leaves**
½ **teaspoon dried oregano leaves**
½ **teaspoon dried basil leaves**
½ **teaspoon black pepper**
2 **pounds top round London broil (1½ inches thick)**
1 **medium red onion, cut into ¼-inch-thick slices**
1 **package (8 ounces) sliced mushrooms**
1 **medium red bell pepper, cut into strips**
1 **medium zucchini, cut into ¼-inch-thick slices**

1. Combine olive oil, wine, shallots, vinegar, garlic, marjoram, oregano, basil and pepper in medium bowl; whisk to blend.

2. Combine London broil and ¾ cup marinade in large resealable plastic food storage bag. Seal bag and turn to coat. Marinate in refrigerator up to 24 hours, turning once or twice.

3. Combine onion, mushrooms, bell pepper, zucchini and remaining marinade in separate large food storage bag. Seal bag and turn to coat. Marinate in refrigerator up to 24 hours, turning once or twice.

4. Preheat broiler. Remove meat from marinade and place on broiler pan; discard marinade. Broil 4 to 5 inches from heat about 9 minutes per side or until desired doneness. Let stand 10 minutes. Cut meat into thin slices.

5. While meat is standing, drain marinade from vegetables and arrange on broiler pan. Broil 4 to 5 inches from heat about 9 minutes or until edges of vegetables just begin to brown. Serve meat and vegetables immediately.

Nutrients per Serving:
Calories: 324 (44% of calories from fat), Carbohydrate: 8g, Total Fat: 16g, Protein: 36g, Cholesterol: 75mg, Sodium: 66mg, Fiber: 2g

London Broil with Marinated Vegetables

The Definitive Steak

Makes 4 servings

4 New York strip steaks (about 5 ounces each)
¼ cup olive oil
2 teaspoons minced garlic
1 teaspoon salt
½ teaspoon black pepper

1. Place steaks in shallow glass container. Combine oil, garlic, salt and pepper in small bowl; mix well. Pour oil mixture over steaks; turn to coat well. Cover; marinate in refrigerator 30 to 60 minutes.

2. Prepare grill for direct cooking.

3. Place steaks on grid. Grill, covered, over medium-high heat 14 minutes for medium, 20 minutes for well or according to desired doneness, turning halfway through grilling time.

Nutrients per Serving:
Calories: 347 (60% of calories from fat), Carbohydrate: 1g, Total Fat: 23g, Protein: 32g, Cholesterol: 66mg, Sodium: 596mg, Fiber: <1g

Food Fact

Olive oil is produced when tree-ripened olives are pressed. Both extra-virgin and virgin oils are cold-pressed from the first pressing of the olives. Extra-virgin is more expensive, with a lower acidity and full-bodied fruity flavor. Oils labeled simply "olive oil" are less expenvie blends with a simpler flavor, making them an economical choice for most uses. Light olive oil is filtered to produce a lighter color and flavor.

Fragrant Beef with Garlic Sauce

Makes 4 servings

1 boneless beef top sirloin steak (about 1¼ pounds)
⅓ cup reduced-sodium teriyaki sauce
10 large cloves garlic, peeled
½ cup fat-free reduced-sodium beef broth
4 cups hot cooked white rice (optional)

1. Place beef and teriyaki sauce in large resealable plastic food storage bag. Seal bag securely; turn to coat. Marinate in refrigerator 30 minutes or up to 4 hours.

2. Combine garlic and broth in small saucepan. Bring to a boil over high heat. Reduce heat to medium. Simmer, uncovered, 5 minutes. Cover and simmer 8 to 9 minutes until garlic is softened. Transfer to blender or food processor; process until smooth.

3. Meanwhile, drain beef; reserve marinade. Place beef on rack of broiler pan. Brush with half of reserved marinade. Broil 5 to 6 inches from heat 6 minutes. Turn beef over; brush with remaining marinade. Broil 6 minutes more.*

4. Slice beef thinly; serve with garlic sauce and rice, if desired.

*Broiling time is for medium-rare doneness. Adjust time for desired doneness.

Nutrients per Serving:
Calories: 212 (24% of calories from fat), Carbohydrate: 6g, Total Fat: 6g, Protein: 33g, Cholesterol: 67mg, Sodium: 1106mg, Fiber: <1g

Poultry

Jalapeño-Lime Chicken

Makes 8 servings

8 chicken thighs
3 tablespoons jalapeño jelly
1 tablespoon olive oil
1 tablespoon lime juice
1 clove garlic, minced
1 teaspoon chili powder
½ teaspoon black pepper
⅛ teaspoon salt

1. Preheat oven to 400°F. Line 15×10-inch jelly-roll pan with foil; spray with nonstick cooking spray.

2. Arrange chicken in single layer in prepared pan. Bake 15 minutes; drain off juices. Combine jelly, oil, lime juice, garlic, chili powder, pepper and salt in small bowl. Turn chicken; brush with half of jelly mixture. Bake 20 minutes. Turn chicken; brush with remaining jelly mixture. Bake 10 to 15 minutes or until juices run clear (180°F).

3. Garnish as desired.

Nutrients per Serving:
Calories: 467 (77% of calories from fat), Carbohydrate: 11g, Total Fat: 32g, Protein: 33g, Cholesterol: 158mg, Sodium: 221mg, Fiber: <1g

Chicken Breasts with Orange Basil Pesto

Makes 6 servings

½ **cup fresh basil leaves**
2 **tablespoons grated orange peel**
2 **cloves garlic**
2 **teaspoons olive oil**
3 **tablespoons Florida orange juice**
1 **tablespoon Dijon-style mustard**
   Salt and pepper to taste
6 **chicken breast halves**

Preheat broiler. Add basil, orange peel and garlic to food processor; process until finely chopped. Add oil, orange juice, mustard, salt and pepper; process a few seconds or until paste forms. Spread equal amounts mixture under skin and on bone side of each chicken breast. Place chicken skin-side down on broiler pan and place 4 inches from heat. Broil 10 minutes. Turn chicken over and broil 10 to 12 minutes or until chicken is no longer pink in center. If chicken browns too quickly, cover with foil. Remove skin from chicken before serving.

Favorite recipe from Florida Department of Citrus

Nutrients per Serving:
Calories: 206 (25% of calories from fat), Carbohydrate: 3g, Total Fat: 6g, Protein: 34g, Cholesterol: 91mg, Sodium: 113mg, Fiber: <1g

Food Fact

During the winter months, fresh basil can be found in small plastic packages in the produce section of the supermarket. Place the basil, stems down, in a glass of water with a plastic bag over the leaves; refrigerate for up to a week, changing the water occasionally.

Chicken Breast with Orange Basil Pesto

Mexican Tortilla Soup

Makes 8 servings

Nonstick cooking spray
2 pounds boneless skinless chicken breasts, cut into ½-inch strips
4 cups diced carrots
2 cups sliced celery
1 cup chopped green bell pepper
1 cup chopped onion
4 cloves garlic, minced
1 jalapeño pepper,* seeded and sliced
1 teaspoon dried oregano leaves
½ teaspoon ground cumin
8 cups fat-free reduced-sodium chicken broth
1 large tomato, seeded and chopped
4 to 5 tablespoons lime juice
2 (6-inch) corn tortillas, cut into ¼-inch strips
Salt (optional)
3 tablespoons finely chopped fresh cilantro

*Jalapeño peppers can sting and irritate the skin; wear rubber gloves when handling peppers and do not touch eyes. Wash hands after handling.

1. Preheat oven to 350°F. Spray large nonstick Dutch oven with cooking spray; heat over medium heat. Add chicken; cook and stir about 10 minutes or until browned and no longer pink in center. Add carrots, celery, bell pepper, onion, garlic, jalapeño pepper, oregano and cumin; cook and stir over medium heat 5 minutes.

2. Stir in chicken broth, tomato and lime juice; heat to a boil. Reduce heat to low; cover and simmer 15 to 20 minutes.

3. Spray tortilla strips lightly with cooking spray; sprinkle very lightly with salt, if desired. Place on baking sheet. Bake about 10 minutes or until browned and crisp, stirring occasionally.

4. Stir cilantro into soup. Ladle soup into bowls; top evenly with tortilla strips.

Nutrients per Serving:
Calories: 184 (15% of calories from fat), Carbohydrate: 16g, Total Fat: 3g, Protein: 23g, Cholesterol: 58mg, Sodium: 132mg, Fiber: 4g

Mexican Tortilla Soup

Turkey Cutlets with Victory Garden Gravy

Makes 4 servings

1 package BUTTERBALL® Fresh Boneless Turkey Breast Cutlets
½ **cup milk**
3 **tablespoons flour**
1 **can (14½ ounces) chicken broth**
2 **cups broccoli florets**
½ **cup chopped plum tomatoes**
1 **tablespoon chopped fresh parsley**
¼ **teaspoon salt**
¼ **teaspoon black pepper**
1 **tablespoon vegetable oil**
2 **tablespoons grated Parmesan cheese**

Whisk together milk and flour in small bowl. Combine milk mixture and chicken broth in large saucepan. Bring to a boil over medium-high heat, stirring constantly. Reduce heat to low; add broccoli. Simmer 5 minutes. Stir in tomatoes, parsley, salt and pepper. Heat oil in separate large skillet over medium heat until hot. Cook cutlets 2 to 2½ minutes on each side or until no longer pink in center. Serve with gravy. Sprinkle with Parmesan cheese.

Preparation Time: 15 minutes

Nutrients per Serving:
Calories: 197 (14% of calories from fat), Carbohydrate: 10g, Total Fat: 3.5g, Protein: 25g, Cholesterol: 49mg, Sodium: 730mg, Fiber: 2g

Japanese Yakitori

Makes 6 servings

1 pound boneless skinless chicken breast halves, cut into ¾-inch-wide strips
2 tablespoons sherry or pineapple juice
2 tablespoons reduced-sodium soy sauce
1 tablespoon sugar
1 tablespoon peanut oil
½ teaspoon minced garlic
½ teaspoon minced ginger
5 ounces red pearl onions
½ fresh pineapple, cut into 1-inch wedges

1. Place chicken in large resealable plastic food storage bag. Combine sherry, soy sauce, sugar, oil, garlic and ginger in small bowl; mix thoroughly to dissolve sugar. Pour into plastic bag with chicken; seal bag and turn to coat thoroughly. Marinate in refrigerator 30 minutes or up to 2 hours, turning occasionally.

2. Meanwhile, place onions in boiling water for 4 minutes; drain and cool in ice water to stop cooking. Cut off root ends and slip off outer skins; set aside.

3. Drain chicken, reserving marinade. Weave chicken accordion-style onto skewers*, alternating onions and pineapple with chicken. Brush with reserved marinade; discard remaining marinade.

4. Grill on uncovered grill over medium-hot coals 6 to 8 minutes or until chicken is no longer pink in center, turning once.

If using wooden skewers, soak skewers in water 20 to 30 minutes to prevent burning.

Nutrients per Serving:
Calories: 124 (21% of calories from fat), Carbohydrate: 6g, Total Fat: 3g, Protein: 17g, Cholesterol: 46mg, Sodium: 99mg, Fiber: 1g

Broccoli-Filled Chicken Roulade

Makes 8 servings

2 cups broccoli florets
1 tablespoon water
¼ cup fresh parsley
1 cup diced red bell pepper
4 ounces fat-free cream cheese, softened
2 tablespoons grated Parmesan cheese
2 tablespoons lemon juice
2 tablespoons olive oil
1 teaspoon paprika
¼ teaspoon salt
1 egg
½ cup fat-free (skim) milk
4 cups cornflakes, crushed
1 tablespoon dried basil leaves
8 boneless skinless chicken breast halves

1. Place broccoli and water in microwavable dish; cover. Microwave at HIGH (100%) 2 minutes. Let stand, covered, 2 minutes. Drain water from broccoli. Place broccoli in food processor or blender. Add parsley; process 10 seconds, scraping side of bowl if necessary. Add bell pepper, cream cheese, Parmesan cheese, lemon juice, oil, paprika and salt. Pulse 2 to 3 times or until bell pepper is minced.

2. Preheat oven to 375°F. Spray 11×7-inch baking pan with nonstick cooking spray. Lightly beat egg in small bowl. Add milk; blend well. Combine cornflake crumbs and basil in shallow bowl.

3. Pound chicken breasts between two pieces of plastic wrap to ¼-inch thickness using flat side of meat mallet or rolling pin. Spread each chicken breast with ⅛ of the broccoli mixture to within ½ inch of edges. Roll up chicken breast from short end, tucking in sides if possible; secure with toothpicks. Dip roulades in milk mixture; roll in cornflake crumb mixture. Place in prepared baking pan. Bake 20 minutes or until chicken is no longer pink in center and juices run clear. Remove toothpicks before serving. Garnish if desired.

Nutrients per Serving:
Calories: 269 (27% of calories from fat), Carbohydrate: 15g, Total Fat: 8g, Protein: 33g, Cholesterol: 103mg, Sodium: 407mg, Fiber: 2g

Broccoli-Filled Chicken Roulade

Coq au Vin

Makes 4 servings

2 slices bacon, cut into ½-inch pieces
1 chicken, cut up (3½ pounds)
1 cup mushrooms, halved
1 red bell pepper, coarsely chopped
1 medium onion, coarsely chopped
¾ cup red wine or dry white wine
1 cup chicken broth, divided
2 cloves garlic, minced
1 teaspoon dried thyme leaves
¼ teaspoon black pepper
¼ cup all-purpose flour
   Chopped parsely (optional)
   Hot cooked rice or noodles

1. Cook bacon in large skillet or Dutch oven over medium heat until crisp. Remove with slotted spoon; set aside.

2. Add chicken pieces to skillet; cook 10 minutes or until golden brown, turning occasionally to brown evenly.

3. Add mushrooms, bell pepper, onion, wine, ¾ cup chicken broth, garlic, thyme and black pepper; bring to a boil. Reduce heat; simmer, covered, 25 minutes.

4. Combine remaining ¼ cup broth and flour; stir until smooth. Stir into chicken mixture. Continue simmering, uncovered, 5 minutes or until thickened. Season to taste with salt and black pepper. Top with reserved bacon and chopped parsley, if desired. Serve with rice.

Nutrients per Serving:
Calories: 517 (38% of calories from fat), Carbohydrate: 16g, Total Fat: 22g, Protein: 54g, Cholesterol: 155mg, Sodium: 413mg, Fiber: 2g

Balsamic Chicken

Makes 6 servings

     6 boneless skinless chicken breast halves
1½ teaspoons fresh rosemary, minced, *or* ½ teaspoon dried rosemary leaves
     2 cloves garlic, minced
¾ teaspoon black pepper
½ teaspoon salt
     1 tablespoon olive oil
¼ cup balsamic vinegar

1. Rinse chicken and pat dry. Combine rosemary, garlic, pepper and salt in small bowl; mix well. Place chicken in large bowl; drizzle chicken with oil and rub with spice mixture. Cover and refrigerate overnight.

2. Preheat oven to 450°F. Spray heavy roasting pan or iron skillet with nonstick cooking spray. Place chicken in pan; bake 10 minutes. Turn chicken over, stirring in 3 to 4 tablespoons water if drippings begin to stick to pan.

3. Bake about 10 minutes or until chicken is golden brown and no longer pink in center. If pan is dry, stir in another 1 to 2 tablespoons water to loosen drippings.

4. Drizzle balsamic vinegar over chicken in pan. Transfer chicken to plates. Stir liquid in pan; drizzle over chicken. Garnish, if desired.

Nutrients per Serving:
Calories: 174 (29% of calories from fat), Carbohydrate: 3g, Total Fat: 5g, Protein: 27g, Cholesterol: 73mg, Sodium: 242mg, Fiber: 1g, Saturated Fat: 1g

Roast Turkey Breast with Spinach-Blue Cheese Stuffing

Makes 14 servings (3 ounces each)

1 frozen whole boneless turkey breast, thawed (3½ to 4 pounds)
1 package (10 ounces) frozen chopped spinach, thawed and squeezed dry
2 ounces blue cheese or feta cheese
2 ounces reduced-fat cream cheese
½ cup finely chopped green onions
4½ teaspoons dried basil leaves
4½ teaspoons Dijon mustard
2 teaspoons dried oregano leaves
Black pepper to taste
Paprika

1. Preheat oven to 350°F. Coat roasting pan and rack with nonstick cooking spray.

2. Unroll turkey breast; rinse and pat dry. Place between 2 sheets of plastic wrap. Pound turkey breast with flat side of meat mallet to about 1-inch thickness. Remove and discard skin from one half of turkey breast; turn meat over so skin side (on other half) faces down.

3. Combine spinach, blue cheese, cream cheese, green onions, basil, mustard and oregano in medium bowl; mix well. Spread evenly over turkey breast. Roll up turkey so skin is on top.

4. Carefully place turkey breast on rack; sprinkle with pepper and paprika. Roast 1½ hours or until no longer pink in center of breast. Remove from oven; let stand 10 minutes before removing skin and slicing. Cut into ¼-inch slices.

Nutrients per Serving:
Calories: 135 (28% of calories from fat), Carbohydrate: 2g, Total Fat: 4g, Protein: 22g, Cholesterol: 50mg, Sodium: 144mg, Fiber: 1g

Chicken Teriyaki

Makes 4 servings

8 large chicken drumsticks (about 2 pounds)
⅓ cup teriyaki sauce
2 tablespoons brandy or apple juice
1 green onion, minced
1 tablespoon vegetable oil
1 teaspoon ground ginger
½ teaspoon sugar
¼ teaspoon garlic powder
   Prepared sweet-and-sour sauce (optional)

1. Remove skin from drumsticks, if desired, by pulling skin toward end of leg using paper towel; discard skin.

2. Place chicken in large resealable plastic food storage bag. Combine teriyaki sauce, brandy, onion, oil, ginger, sugar and garlic powder in small bowl; pour over chicken. Close bag securely, turn to coat. Marinate in refrigerator at least 1 hour or overnight, turning occasionally.

3. Prepare grill for indirect cooking.

4. Drain chicken; reserve marinade. Place chicken on grid directly over drip pan. Grill, covered, over medium-high heat 60 minutes or until chicken is no longer pink in center and juices run clear, turning and brushing with reserved marinade every 20 minutes. *Do not brush with marinade during last 5 minutes of grilling.* Discard remaining marinade. Serve with sweet-and-sour sauce, if desired.

Nutrients per Serving:
Calories: 224 (32% of calories from fat), Carbohydrate: 5g, Total Fat: 8g, Protein: 26g, Cholesterol: 82mg, Sodium: 1003mg, Fiber: <1g

Chicken Roll-Ups

Makes 4 servings

¼ **cup fresh lemon juice**
1 **tablespoon olive oil**
¼ **teaspoon salt**
¼ **teaspoon black pepper**
4 **boneless skinless chicken breast halves**
¼ **cup finely chopped fresh Italian parsley**
2 **tablespoons grated Parmesan cheese**
2 **tablespoons chopped fresh chives**
1 **teaspoon finely grated lemon peel**
2 **large cloves garlic, pressed in garlic press**
16 **toothpicks soaked in hot water 15 minutes**

1. Combine lemon juice, oil, salt and pepper in 11×7-inch casserole. Pound chicken to ⅜-inch thickness. Place chicken in lemon mixture; turn to coat. Cover; marinate in refrigerator at least 30 minutes.

2. Prepare grill for direct cooking.

3. Combine parsley, cheese, chives, lemon peel and garlic in small bowl. Discard chicken marinade. Spread ¼ of parsley mixture over each chicken breast, to within 1 inch of edges. Starting at narrow end, roll chicken to enclose filling; secure with toothpicks.

4. Grill chicken, covered, over medium-hot coals about 2 minutes on each side or until golden brown. Transfer chicken to low or indirect heat; grill, covered, about 5 minutes or until chicken is no longer pink in center.

5. Remove toothpicks; slice each chicken breast into 3 or 4 pieces.

Nutrients per Serving:
Calories: 159 (24% of calories from fat), Carbohydrate: 2g, Total Fat: 4g, Protein: 27g, Cholesterol: 69mg, Sodium: 139mg, Fiber: <1g

Broiled Chicken Breasts with Cilantro Salsa

Makes 4 servings

4 small boneless skinless chicken breast halves (4 ounces each)
4 tablespoons lime juice, divided
   Black pepper
½ cup lightly packed fresh cilantro, chopped
⅓ cup thinly sliced or minced green onions
¼ to ½ jalapeño pepper,* seeded and minced
2 tablespoons pine nuts, toasted (optional)

*Jalapeño peppers can sting and irritate the skin. Wear rubber gloves when handling peppers and do not touch eyes. Wash hands after handling.

1. Spray broiler pan or baking sheet with nonstick cooking spray.

2. Brush chicken with 2 tablespoons lime juice. Place on prepared pan. Sprinkle generously with pepper; set aside.

3. Combine remaining 2 tablespoons lime juice, cilantro, onions, jalapeño pepper and pine nuts, if desired, in small bowl; stir to combine. Set aside.

4. Broil chicken 1 to 2 inches from heat 8 to 10 minutes or until chicken is no longer pink in center. Serve with cilantro salsa. Garnish with lime slices, if desired.

Nutrients per Serving:
Calories: 122 (19% of calories from fat), Carbohydrate: 2g, Total Fat: 3g, Protein: 22g, Cholesterol: 58mg, Sodium: 80mg, Fiber: 1g

Easy Chicken Salad

Makes 2 servings

¼ **cup finely diced celery**
¼ **cup reduced-fat mayonnaise**
2 **tablespoons sweet pickle relish**
1 **tablespoon minced onion**
½ **teaspoon Dijon mustard**
⅛ **teaspoon salt**
   Black pepper
2 **cups cubed cooked chicken**
   Salad greens

1. Combine celery, mayonnaise, relish, onion, mustard, salt and pepper in medium bowl; mix well. Stir in chicken. Cover; refrigerate at least 1 hour.

2. Serve on salad greens with fruit, if desired.

Nutrients per Serving:
Calories: 410 (44% of calories from fat), Carbohydrate: 16g, Total Fat: 20g, Protein: 41g, Cholesterol: 130mg, Sodium: 790mg, Fiber: 1g

Food Fact

Two whole chicken breasts (about 10 ounces each) will yield about 2 cups of chopped cooked chicken; one broiling/frying chicken (about 3 pounds) will yield about 2-1/2 cups chopped cooked chicken.

Turkey Piccata

Makes 4 servings

⅓ **cup all-purpose flour**
½ **teaspoon salt**
½ **teaspoon black pepper**
 1 **boneless turkey breast (1 pound), cut into 4 slices**
 3 **tablespoons olive oil, divided**
1½ **cups sliced fresh mushrooms**
 2 **cloves garlic, crushed**
½ **cup chicken broth**
 2 **tablespoons lemon juice**
½ **teaspoon dried oregano leaves**
 3 **tablespoons pine nuts**
 2 **tablespoons chopped fresh parsley**

1. Combine flour, salt and pepper in resealable plastic food storage bag. Add turkey; shake to evenly coat with flour mixture. Set aside.

2. Heat 2 tablespoons oil in large skillet over medium-high heat until hot. Add turkey; cook 3 minutes on each side or until lightly browned and turkey is no longer pink in center. Remove from skillet to serving plate. Cover with foil and keep warm.

3. Add remaining 1 tablespoon oil to skillet. Heat over medium-high heat until hot. Add mushrooms and garlic. Cook and stir 2 minutes. Add broth, lemon juice and oregano. Bring to a boil. Reduce heat to medium; simmer, uncovered, 3 minutes.

4. Spoon mushroom sauce over turkey. Sprinkle with pine nuts and parsley. Serve immediately.

Nutrients per Serving:
Calories: 287 (53% of calories from fat), Carbohydrate: 12g, Total Fat: 17g, Protein: 23g, Cholesterol: 46mg, Sodium: 433mg, Fiber: 1g

Asian Chicken Kabobs

Makes 4 servings

1 pound boneless skinless chicken breasts, cut into 1½-inch pieces
2 small zucchini or yellow squash, cut into 1-inch slices
8 large fresh mushrooms
1 cup red, yellow or green bell pepper pieces
2 tablespoons reduced-sodium soy sauce
2 tablespoons dry sherry
1 teaspoon dark sesame oil
2 cloves garlic, minced
2 large green onions, cut into 1-inch pieces

1. Place chicken, zucchini, mushrooms and bell pepper in large plastic resealable food storage bag. Combine soy sauce, sherry, oil and garlic in small bowl; pour over chicken and vegetables. Seal bag; turn to coat. Marinate in refrigerator at least 30 minutes or up to 4 hours.

2. Soak 4 (12-inch) skewers in water to cover 20 minutes.

3. Drain chicken and vegetables; reserve marinade. Alternately thread chicken and vegetables with onions onto skewers.

4. Place on rack of broiler pan. Brush with half of reserved marinade. Broil 5 to 6 inches from heat 5 minutes. Turn kabobs over; brush with remaining marinade. Broil 5 minutes or until chicken is no longer pink. Garnish with green onion brushes, if desired.

Nutrients per Serving:
Calories: 135 (21% of calories from fat), Carbohydrate: 6g, Total Fat: 3g, Protein: 19g, Cholesterol: 46mg, Sodium: 307mg, Fiber: 2g

Lemon Pepper Chicken

Makes 4 servings

⅓ cup lemon juice
¼ cup finely chopped onion
¼ cup olive oil
1 tablespoon brown sugar
1 tablespoon cracked black pepper
3 cloves garlic, minced
2 teaspoons grated lemon peel
¾ teaspoon salt
4 chicken quarters (about 2½ pounds)

1. Combine lemon juice, onion, oil, sugar, pepper, garlic, lemon peel and salt in small bowl; reserve 2 tablespoons marinade. Combine remaining marinade and chicken in large resealable plastic food storage bag. Seal bag; turn to coat. Marinate in refrigerator at least 4 hours or overnight.

2. Prepare grill for direct cooking. Remove chicken from marinade; discard marinade. Arrange chicken on microwavable plate; cover with waxed paper. Microwave at HIGH (100%) 5 minutes. Turn and rearrange chicken. Cover and microwave at HIGH 5 minutes.

3. Transfer chicken to grill. Grill covered over medium-hot coals 15 to 20 minutes or until juices run clear, turning several times and basting often with reserved marinade.

Nutrients per Serving:
Calories: 375 (55% of calories from fat), Carbohydrate: 3g, Total Fat: 23g, Protein: 37g, Cholesterol: 129mg, Sodium: 256mg, Fiber: <1g

Chicken Piccata

Makes 4 servings

   3 tablespoons all-purpose flour
   ½ teaspoon salt
   ¼ teaspoon black pepper
   4 boneless skinless chicken breast halves (4 ounces)
   2 teaspoons olive oil
   1 teaspoon butter
   2 cloves garlic, minced
   ¾ cup canned fat-free reduced-sodium chicken broth
   1 tablespoon fresh lemon juice
   2 tablespoons chopped Italian parsley
   1 tablespoon drained capers
      Lemon slices and parsley sprigs (optional)

1. Combine flour, salt and pepper in shallow pie plate. Reserve 1 tablespoon of flour mixture.

2. Place chicken between sheets of plastic wrap or waxed paper; pound to ½-inch thickness. Dredge chicken in remaining flour mixture.

3. Heat oil and butter in large nonstick skillet over medium heat until butter is melted. Add chicken; cook 4 to 5 minutes per side or until chicken is cooked through. Transfer to serving platter; set aside.

4. Add garlic to same skillet; cook and stir over medium heat 1 minute. Add reserved flour mixture; cook 1 minute, stirring constantly. Add broth and lemon juice; simmer, stirring frequently, until sauce thickens, about 2 minutes. Stir in parsley and capers; spoon sauce over chicken. Garnish with lemon slices and parsley sprigs, if desired.

Nutrients per Serving:
Calories: 194 (30% of calories from fat), Carbohydrate: 5g, Total Fat: 6g, Protein: 27g, Cholesterol: 71mg, Sodium: 473mg, Fiber: <1g

Spicy Island Chicken

Makes 6 servings

 1 cup finely chopped white onion
 ⅓ cup white wine vinegar
 6 green onions, finely chopped
 6 cloves garlic, minced
 1 habañero or serrano pepper,* finely chopped
 4½ teaspoons olive oil
 4½ teaspoons fresh thyme leaves *or* 2 teaspoons dried thyme leaves
 1 tablespoon ground allspice
 2 teaspoons sugar
 1 teaspoon salt
 1 teaspoon ground cinnamon
 1 teaspoon ground nutmeg
 1 teaspoon black pepper
 ½ teaspoon ground red pepper
 6 boneless skinless chicken breasts

*Peppers can sting and irritate the skin; wear rubber gloves when handling peppers and do not touch eyes. Wash hands after handling.

1. Combine all ingredients except chicken in medium bowl; mix well. Place chicken in resealable plastic food storage bag and add seasoning mixture. Seal bag; turn to coat. Marinate in refrigerator 4 hours or overnight.

2. Spray cold grid with nonstick cooking spray. Adjust grid to 4 to 6 inches above heat. Preheat grill to medium-high heat.

3. Remove chicken from marinade. Grill 5 to 7 minutes per side or until chicken is no longer pink in center, brushing occasionally with marinade. *Do not brush with marinade during last 5 minutes of grilling.* Discard remaining marinade. Garnish if desired.

Nutrients per Serving:
Calories: 164 (27% of calories from fat), Carbohydrate: 3g, Total Fat: 5g, Protein: 26g, Cholesterol: 69mg, Sodium: 256mg, Fiber: 1g

142

Maple-Glazed Turkey Breast

Makes 6 to 8 servings

1 bone-in turkey breast (5 to 6 pounds)
¼ cup pure maple syrup
2 tablespoons butter or margarine, melted
1 tablespoon bourbon (optional)
2 teaspoons freshly grated orange peel
Fresh bay leaves for garnish

1. Prepare grill with rectangular foil drip pan. Bank briquets on either side of drip pan for indirect cooking.

2. Insert meat thermometer into center of thickest part of turkey breast, not touching bone. Place turkey, bone side down, on roast rack or directly on grid, directly over drip pan. Grill turkey on covered grill over medium coals 55 minutes, adding 4 to 9 briquets to both sides of fire after 45 minutes to maintain medium coals.

3. Combine maple syrup, butter, bourbon, if desired, and orange peel in small bowl; brush half of mixture over turkey. Continue to grill, covered, 10 minutes. Brush with remaining mixture; continue to grill, covered, about 10 minutes or until thermometer registers 170°F.

4. Transfer turkey to carving board; tent with foil. Let stand 10 minutes before carving. Cut turkey into thin slices. Garnish, if desired.

Variation: For hickory-smoked flavor, cover 2 cups hickory chips with cold water; soak 20 minutes. Drain; sprinkle over coals just before placing turkey on grid.

Nutrients per Serving:
Calories: 537 (23% of calories from fat), Carbohydrate: 9g, Total Fat: 13g, Protein: 90g, Cholesterol: 274mg, Sodium: 166mg, Fiber: <1g

Thai Grilled Chicken

Makes 4 servings

4 boneless chicken breast halves, skinned if desired (about 1¼ pounds)
¼ cup soy sauce
2 teaspoons bottled minced garlic
½ teaspoon red pepper flakes
2 tablespoons honey
1 tablespoon fresh lime juice

1. Prepare grill for direct cooking. Place chicken in shallow dish or plate. Combine soy sauce, garlic and pepper flakes in small bowl. Pour over chicken, turn to coat. Marinate in refrigerator 10 minutes.

2. Meanwhile, combine honey and lime juice in small bowl until blended; set aside.

3. Place chicken on grid over medium coals; brush with some of remaining marinade. Discard remaining marinade. Grill over covered grill 5 minutes. Brush chicken with half of honey mixture; turn and brush with remaining honey mixture. Grill 5 minutes more or until chicken is no longer pink in center and juices run clear.

Nutrients per Serving:
Calories: 206 (17% of calories from fat), Carbohydrate: 10g, Total Fat: 4g, Protein: 32g, Cholesterol: 86mg, Sodium: 417mg, Fiber: <1g

Gingered Chicken with Vegetables

Makes 4 servings

2 tablespoons vegetable oil, divided
1 pound boneless skinless chicken breasts, cut into thin strips
1 cup red pepper strips
1 cup sliced fresh mushrooms
16 fresh pea pods, cut in half crosswise
½ cup sliced water chestnuts
¼ cup sliced green onions
1 tablespoon grated fresh gingerroot
1 large clove garlic, crushed
⅔ cup reduced-fat, reduced-sodium chicken broth
2 tablespoons EQUAL® SPOONFUL*
2 tablespoons light soy sauce
4 teaspoons cornstarch
2 teaspoons dark sesame oil
Salt and pepper to taste

May substitute 3 packets Equal® sweetener.

• Heat 1 tablespoon vegetable oil in large skillet over medium-high heat. Stir-fry chicken until no longer pink; remove chicken from skillet. Heat remaining 1 tablespoon vegetable oil in skillet. Add bell peppers, mushrooms, pea pods, water chestnuts, green onions, ginger and garlic to skillet. Stir-fry mixture 3 to 4 minutes until vegetables are crisp-tender.

• Meanwhile, combine chicken broth, Equal®, soy sauce, cornstarch and sesame oil until smooth. Stir into skillet mixture. Cook over medium heat until thick and clear. Stir in chicken; heat through. Season with salt and pepper to taste.

• Serve over hot cooked rice, if desired.

Nutrients per Serving:
Calories: 263 (38% of calories from fat), Carbohydrate: 11g, Total Fat: 11g, Protein: 29g, Cholesterol: 66mg, Sodium: 411mg, Fiber: 2g

Southwest Chicken

Makes 4 servings

2 tablespoons olive oil
1 clove garlic, pressed
1 teaspoon chili powder
1 teaspoon ground cumin
1 teaspoon dried oregano leaves
½ teaspoon salt
1 pound skinless boneless chicken breast halves or thighs

Combine oil, garlic, chili powder, cumin, oregano and salt; brush over both sides of chicken to coat. Grill chicken over medium-hot KINGSFORD® Briquets 8 to 10 minutes or until chicken is no longer pink, turning once. Serve immediately or use in Build a Burrito, Taco Salad or other favorite recipes.

Note: Southwest Chicken can be grilled ahead and refrigerated for several days or frozen for longer storage.

Build a Burrito: Top warm large flour tortillas with strips of Southwest Chicken and your choice of drained canned black beans, cooked brown or white rice, shredded cheese, salsa verde, shredded lettuce, sliced black olives and chopped cilantro. Fold in sides and roll to enclose filling. Heat in microwave oven at HIGH (100%) until heated through. (Or, wrap in foil and heat in preheated 350°F oven.)

Taco Salad: For a quick one-dish meal, layer strips of Southwest Chicken with tomato wedges, blue or traditional corn tortilla chips, sliced black olives, shredded romaine or iceberg lettuce, shredded cheese and avocado slices. Serve with salsa, sour cream, guacamole or a favorite dressing.

Nutrients per Serving:
Calories: 191 (41% of calories from fat), Carbohydrate: 1g, Total Fat: 8g, Protein: 26g, Cholesterol: 66mg, Sodium: 358mg, Fiber: <1g

Chicken Salad

Makes 4 servings

¼ **cup mayonnaise**
¼ **cup sour cream**
1 **tablespoon lemon juice**
1 **teaspoon sugar**
1 **teaspoon grated lemon peel**
1 **teaspoon Dijon mustard**
½ **teaspoon salt**
⅛ **to ¼ teaspoon white pepper**
2 **cups diced cooked chicken**
1 **cup sliced celery**
¼ **cup sliced green onions**
   Lettuce leaves
   Crumbled blue cheese (optional)

1. Combine mayonnaise, sour cream, lemon juice, sugar, lemon peel, mustard, salt and pepper in large bowl.

2. Add chicken, celery and green onions; stir to combine. Cover; refrigerate at least 1 hour to allow flavors to blend.

3. Serve salad on lettuce-lined plate. Sprinkle with blue cheese, if desired.

Nutrients per Serving:
Calories: 310 (67% of calories from fat), Carbohydrate: 4g, Total Fat: 23g, Protein: 22g, Cholesterol: 69mg, Sodium: 442mg, Fiber: 1g

Roast Turkey with Cranberry Stuffing

Makes 20 servings

    1 loaf (12 ounces) Italian or French bread, cut into ½-inch cubes
    2 tablespoons margarine
1½ cups chopped onions
1½ cups chopped celery
    2 teaspoons poultry seasoning
    1 teaspoon dried thyme leaves
    ½ teaspoon dried rosemary, crushed
    ¼ teaspoon salt
    ¼ teaspoon black pepper
    1 cup coarsely chopped fresh cranberries
    1 tablespoon sugar
    ¾ cup fat-free reduced-sodium chicken broth
    1 turkey (8 to 10 pounds)

1. Preheat oven to 375°F.

2. Arrange bread on two 15×10-inch jelly-roll pans. Bake 12 minutes or until lightly toasted. *Reduce oven temperature to 350°F.*

3. Melt margarine in large saucepan over medium heat. Add onions and celery; cook and stir 8 minutes or until vegetables are tender; remove from heat. Add bread cubes, poultry seasoning, thyme, rosemary, salt and pepper; mix well. Combine cranberries and sugar in small bowl; mix well. Add to bread mixture; toss until well blended. Drizzle chicken broth evenly over mixture; toss until well blended.

4. Remove giblets from turkey. Rinse turkey and cavity in cold water; pat dry with paper towels. Fill turkey cavity loosely with stuffing. Place remaining stuffing in casserole sprayed with nonstick cooking spray. Cover stuffing; refrigerate until ready to bake.

5. Spray roasting pan with nonstick cooking spray. Place turkey, breast side up, on rack in roasting pan. Bake 3 hours or until thermometer inserted in thickest part of thigh registers 180°F and juices run clear.

6. Transfer turkey to serving platter. Cover loosely with foil; let stand 20 minutes. Place remaining stuffing in oven; increase temperature to 375°F. Bake 25 to 30 minutes or until hot.

continued on page 156

Roast Turkey with Cranberry Stuffing

Roast Turkey with Cranberry Stuffing, continued

7. Remove and discard turkey skin. Slice turkey and serve with cranberry stuffing. Garnish as desired.

Nutrients per Serving:
Calories: 220 (26% of calories from fat), Carbohydrate: 12g, Total Fat: 6g, Protein: 28g, Cholesterol: 68mg, Sodium: 223mg, Fiber: <1g

Grilled Marinated Chicken

Makes 8 servings

> **8 whole chicken legs (thighs and drumsticks attached) (about 3½ pounds)**
> **6 ounces frozen lemonade concentrate, thawed**
> **2 tablespoons white wine vinegar**
> **1 tablespoon grated lemon peel**
> **2 cloves garlic, minced**

1. Remove skin and all visible fat from chicken. Place chicken in 13×9-inch glass baking dish. Combine remaining ingredients in small bowl; blend well. Pour over chicken; turn to coat. Cover; marinate in refrigerator 3 hours or overnight, turning occasionally.

2. Spray grid with nonstick cooking spray. Prepare coals for grilling.

3. Place chicken on grill 4 inches from medium-hot coals. Grill 20 to 30 minutes or until chicken is no longer pink near bone, turning occasionally. (Do not overcook or chicken will be dry.) Garnish with curly endive and lemon peel strips, if desired.

Nutrients per Serving:
Calories: 169 (38% of calories from fat), Carbohydrate: 3g, Total Fat: 7g, Protein: 22g, Cholesterol: 77mg, Sodium: 75mg, Fiber: <1g

Quick Orange Chicken

Makes 4 servings

2 tablespoons frozen orange juice concentrate
1 tablespoon no-sugar-added orange marmalade
1 teaspoon Dijon mustard
¼ teaspoon salt
4 boneless skinless chicken breasts (about 1 pound)
½ cup fresh orange sections
2 tablespoons chopped fresh parsley

Microwave Directions

1. For sauce, combine juice concentrate, marmalade, mustard and salt in 8-inch shallow round microwavable dish until juice concentrate is thawed.

2. Add chicken, coating both sides with sauce. Arrange chicken around edge of dish without overlapping. Cover with vented plastic wrap. Microwave at HIGH (100%) 3 minutes; turn chicken over. Microwave at MEDIUM-HIGH (70% power) 4 minutes or until chicken is no longer pink in center.

3. Remove chicken to serving plate. Microwave remaining sauce at HIGH (100%) 2 to 3 minutes or until slightly thickened.

4. To serve, spoon sauce over chicken; top with orange sections and parsley.

Nutrients per Serving:
Calories: 157 (16% of calories from fat), Carbohydrate: 10g, Total Fat: 3g, Protein: 23g, Cholesterol: 60mg, Sodium: 207mg, Fiber: 1g

Chili Turkey Loaf

Makes 8 servings

2 pounds ground turkey
1 cup chopped onion
⅔ cup Italian-style seasoned dry bread crumbs
½ cup chopped green bell pepper
½ cup chili sauce
2 eggs, lightly beaten
2 tablespoons horseradish mustard
4 cloves garlic, minced
1 teaspoon salt
½ teaspoon dried Italian seasoning
¼ teaspoon black pepper
   Prepared salsa (optional)

Slow Cooker Directions

Make foil handles for loaf using technique described below. Mix all ingredients except salsa in large bowl. Shape into round loaf and place on foil strips. Transfer to bottom of slow cooker using foil handles. Cover and cook on LOW 4½ to 5 hours or until juices run clear and temperature is 170°F. Remove loaf from slow cooker using foil handles. Place on serving plate. Let stand 5 minutes before serving. Cut into wedges and top with salsa, if desired. Serve with steamed carrots, if desired.

Foil Handles: Tear off three 18×2-inch strips of heavy foil or use regular foil folded to double thickness. Crisscross foil strips in spoke design and place in slow cooker to allow for easy removal of turkey loaf.

Nutrients per Serving:
Calories: 263 (44% of calories from fat), Carbohydrate: 12g, Total Fat: 13g, Protein: 23g, Cholesterol: 110mg, Sodium: 733mg, Fiber: 1g

Sassy Chicken & Peppers

Makes 2 servings

2 teaspoons Mexican seasoning*
2 boneless skinless chicken breasts (4 ounces each)
2 teaspoons canola oil
1 small red onion, sliced
½ red bell pepper, cut into long, thin strips
½ yellow or green bell pepper, cut into long, thin strips
¼ cup chunky salsa or chipotle salsa
1 tablespoon lime juice
   Lime wedges (optional)

If Mexican seasoning is not available, substitute 1 teaspoon chili powder, $1/2$ teaspoon ground cumin, $1/2$ teaspoon salt and $1/8$ teaspoon ground red pepper.

1. Sprinkle seasoning over both sides of chicken.

2. Heat oil in large nonstick skillet over medium heat. Add onion; cook 3 minutes, stirring occasionally.

3. Add bell pepper strips; cook 3 minutes, stirring occasionally.

4. Push vegetables to edges of skillet; add chicken to skillet. Cook 5 minutes; turn. Stir salsa and lime juice into vegetables. Continue to cook 4 minutes or until chicken is no longer pink in center and vegetables are tender.

5. Transfer chicken to serving plates; top with vegetable mixture and garnish with lime wedges, if desired.

Nutrients per Serving:
Calories: 224 (31% of calories from fat), Carbohydrate: 11g, Total Fat: 8g, Protein: 27g, Cholesterol: 69mg, Sodium: 813mg, Fiber: 3g

Turkey Teriyaki with Grilled Mushrooms

Makes 4 servings

1¼ pounds turkey breast slices, tenderloins or medallions
¼ cup sake or sherry wine
¼ cup soy sauce
3 tablespoons granulated sugar, brown sugar or honey
1 piece (1-inch cube) fresh ginger, minced
3 cloves garlic, minced
1 tablespoon vegetable oil
½ pound mushrooms
4 green onions, cut into 2-inch pieces

Cut turkey slices into long 2-inch-wide strips.* Combine sake, soy sauce, sugar, ginger, garlic and oil in 2-quart glass dish. Add turkey; turn to coat. Cover and refrigerate 15 minutes or overnight. Remove turkey from marinade; discard marinade. Thread turkey onto metal or wooden skewers, alternating with mushrooms and green onions. (Soak wooden skewers in hot water 30 minutes to prevent burning.) Grill on covered grill over medium-hot KINGSFORD® Briquets about 3 minutes per side until turkey is cooked through.

*Do not cut tenderloins or medallions.

Nutrients per Serving:
Calories: 184 (7% of calories from fat), Carbohydrate: 4g, Total Fat: 1g, Protein: 37g, Cholesterol: 88mg, Sodium: 160mg, Fiber: 1g

Turkey Teriyaki with Grilled Mushrooms

Chicken Breasts Smothered in Tomatoes and Mozzarella

Makes 4 servings

4 boneless skinless chicken breast halves (about 1½ pounds)
3 tablespoons olive oil, divided
1 cup chopped onions
2 teaspoons bottled minced garlic
1 can (14 ounces) Italian-style stewed tomatoes
1½ cups (6 ounces) shredded mozzarella cheese

1. Preheat broiler.

2. Pound chicken breasts between 2 pieces of plastic wrap to ¼-inch thickness using flat side of meat mallet or rolling pin.

3. Heat 2 tablespoons oil in ovenproof skillet over medium heat. Add chicken and cook about 3½ minutes per side or until no longer pink in center. Transfer to plate; cover and keep warm.

4. Heat remaining 1 tablespoon oil in same skillet over medium heat. Add onions and garlic; cook and stir 3 minutes. Add tomatoes; bring to a simmer. Return chicken to skillet, spooning onion and tomato mixture over chicken.

5. Sprinkle cheese over top. Broil 4 to 5 inches from heat until cheese is melted.

Nutrients per Serving:
Calories: 442 (43% of calories from fat), Carbohydrate: 11g, Total Fat: 21g, Protein: 51g, Cholesterol: 121mg, Sodium: 563mg, Fiber: 1.5g

Roast Chicken with Peppers

Makes 6 servings

 1 chicken (3 to 3½ pounds), cut into pieces
 3 tablespoons olive oil, divided
1½ tablespoons chopped fresh rosemary *or* 1½ teaspoons dried rosemary, crushed
 1 tablespoon fresh lemon juice
1¼ teaspoons salt, divided
 ¾ teaspoon black pepper, divided
 3 bell peppers (preferably 1 red, 1 yellow and 1 green)
 1 medium onion

1. Preheat oven to 375°F. Rinse chicken in cold water; pat dry with paper towels. Place in shallow roasting pan.

2. Combine 2 tablespoons oil, rosemary and lemon juice; brush over chicken. Sprinkle 1 teaspoon salt and ½ teaspoon pepper over chicken. Roast 15 minutes.

3. Cut bell peppers lengthwise into ½-inch-thick strips. Slice onion into thin wedges. Toss vegetables with remaining 1 tablespoon oil, ¼ teaspoon salt and ¼ teaspoon pepper. Spoon vegetables around chicken; roast until vegetables are tender and chicken is no longer pink in center, about 40 minutes. Serve chicken with vegetables and pan juices.

Nutrients per Serving:
Calories: 428 (67% of calories from fat), Carbohydrate: 6g, Total Fat: 32g, Protein: 29g, Cholesterol: 118mg, Sodium: 575mg, Fiber: 2g

Chicken Provençal

Makes 6 servings

1 tablespoon olive oil
2 pounds skinless chicken thighs
½ cup sliced green bell pepper
½ cup sliced onion
2 cloves garlic, minced
1 pound eggplant, peeled and cut into ¼-inch-thick slices
2 medium tomatoes, cut into ¼-inch-thick slices
¼ cup chopped fresh parsley *or* 2 teaspoons dried parsley
¼ cup chopped fresh basil *or* 2 teaspoons dried basil leaves
1 teaspoon salt
1 cup fat-free reduced-sodium chicken broth
½ cup dry white wine

1. Heat oil in large skillet over medium-high heat. Add chicken; cook 2 to 3 minutes on each side or until browned. Remove chicken.

2. Add bell pepper, onion and garlic to same skillet; cook and stir 3 to 4 minutes or until onion is tender.

3. Return chicken to skillet. Arrange eggplant and tomato slices over chicken. Sprinkle with parsley, basil and salt. Add chicken broth and wine; bring to a boil. Reduce heat; cover and simmer 45 to 50 minutes or until chicken is no longer pink and juices run clear.

Nutrients per Serving:
Calories: 216 (42% of calories from fat), Carbohydrate: 10g, Total Fat: 10g, Protein: 19g, Cholesterol: 62mg, Sodium: 478mg, Fiber: 3g

Turkey with Mustard Sauce

Makes 4 servings

1 tablespoon butter or margarine
1 pound turkey cutlets
1 cup BIRDS EYE® frozen Mixed Vegetables
1 box (9 ounces) BIRDS EYE® frozen Pearl Onions in Cream Sauce
1 teaspoon spicy brown mustard

• In large nonstick skillet, melt butter over medium-high heat. Add turkey; cook until browned on both sides.

• Add mixed vegetables, onions with cream sauce and mustard; bring to boil. Reduce heat to medium-low; cover and simmer 6 to 8 minutes or until vegetables are tender and turkey is no longer pink in center.

Serving Suggestion: Serve with a fresh garden salad.

Prep Time: 5 minutes
Cook Time: 15 minutes

Nutrients per Serving:
Calories: 218 (20% of calories from fat), Carbohydrate: 7g, Total Fat: 5g, Protein: 35g, Cholesterol: 105mg, Sodium: 299mg, Fiber: 1g

Food Fact *Prepared mustard is a pungent, hot condiment made from ground seeds of the same plant that produces mustard greens. The seeds are mixed with vinegar, water or wine and a variety of spices to make prepared mustard.*

Chicken Parmesan

Makes 6 servings

½ cup Italian-seasoned dried bread crumbs
1 teaspoon dried basil leaves
1 teaspoon dried oregano leaves
6 boneless skinless chicken breast halves
½ cup reduced-fat (2%) milk
1 tablespoon olive oil
½ cup (2 ounces) grated Parmesan cheese
1 jar (26 ounces) marinara sauce
1½ cups (6 ounces) shredded part-skim mozzarella cheese

1. Preheat oven to 350°F. Combine bread crumbs, basil and oregano in small bowl. Dip chicken in milk. Dredge coated chicken in bread crumb mixture.

2. Heat oil in large skillet over medium-high heat until hot. Add chicken and cook 2 to 3 minutes on each side or until browned.

3. Place chicken in 13×9-inch baking dish coated with nonstick cooking spray. Sprinkle Parmesan cheese over chicken. Pour marinara sauce over chicken and top with mozzarella cheese. Bake, covered, 45 minutes or until chicken is no longer pink in center.

Nutrients per Serving:
Calories: 317 (42% of calories from fat), Carbohydrate: 15g, Total Fat: 14g, Protein: 30g, Cholesterol: 66mg, Sodium: 946mg, Fiber: 2g

Pork

Margarita Pork Kabobs

Makes 4 servings

1 cup margarita drink mix *or* 1 cup lime juice, 4 teaspoons sugar and ½ teaspoon salt
1 teaspoon ground coriander
1 clove garlic, minced
1 pound pork tenderloin, cut into 1-inch cubes
2 tablespoons margarine, melted
1 tablespoon minced fresh parsley
2 teaspoons lime juice
⅛ teaspoon sugar
1 large green or red bell pepper, cut into 1-inch cubes
2 ears corn, cut into 8 pieces

For marinade, combine margarita mix, coriander and garlic in small bowl. Place pork cubes in large resealable plastic food storage bag; pour marinade over pork. Close bag securely; turn to coat. Marinate for at least 30 minutes. Combine margarine, parsley, lime juice and sugar in small bowl; set aside. Thread pork cubes onto four skewers, alternating with pieces of bell pepper and corn. (If using bamboo skewers, soak in water 20 to 30 minutes before using to prevent them from burning.) Grill over hot coals for 15 to 20 minutes or until barely pink in center, basting with margarine mixture and turning frequently.

Favorite recipe from National Pork Board

Nutrients per Serving:
Calories: 240 (37% of calories from fat), Carbohydrate: 13g, Total Fat: 10g, Protein: 25g, Cholesterol: 66mg, Sodium: 129mg, Fiber: 1g

Mustard-Crusted Roast Pork

Makes 8 servings

3 tablespoons Dijon mustard
4 teaspoons minced garlic, divided
2 whole well-trimmed pork tenderloins (about 1 pound each)
2 tablespoons dried thyme leaves
1 teaspoon black pepper
½ teaspoon salt
1 pound asparagus spears, ends trimmed
2 red or yellow bell peppers (or one of each), cut lengthwise into ½-inch-wide strips
1 cup fat-free reduced-sodium chicken broth, divided

1. Preheat oven to 375°F. Combine mustard and 3 teaspoons garlic in small bowl. Place tenderloins on waxed paper; spread mustard mixture evenly over top and sides of both tenderloins. Combine thyme, black pepper and salt in small bowl; reserve 1 teaspoon mixture. Sprinkle remaining mixture evenly over tenderloins, patting so that seasoning adheres to mustard. Place tenderloins on rack in shallow roasting pan. Roast 25 minutes.

2. Arrange asparagus and bell peppers in single layer in shallow casserole or 13×9-inch baking pan. Add ¼ cup broth, reserved thyme mixture and remaining 1 teaspoon garlic; toss to coat.

3. Roast vegetables in oven, alongside pork tenderloins, 15 to 20 minutes or until thermometer inserted into center of pork registers 160°F and vegetables are tender. Transfer tenderloins to carving board; tent with foil and let stand 5 minutes. Arrange vegetables on serving platter, reserving juices in dish; cover and keep warm. Add remaining ¾ cup broth and juices in dish to roasting pan. Place over range-top burner(s); simmer 3 to 4 minutes over medium-high heat or until juices are reduced to ¾ cup, stirring frequently. Carve tenderloin crosswise into ¼-inch-thick slices; arrange on serving platter. Spoon juices over tenderloin and vegetables.

Nutrients per Serving:
Calories: 182 (23% of calories from fat), Carbohydrate: 8g, Total Fat: 5g, Protein: 27g, Cholesterol: 65mg, Sodium: 304mg, Fiber: 1g

Pork Chops Paprikash

Makes 4 servings

2 teaspoons butter
1 medium onion, very thinly sliced crosswise
1¼ teaspoons paprika, divided
1 teaspoon garlic salt
½ teaspoon black pepper
4 (5- to 6-ounce) bone-in center-cut pork chops (about ½ inch thick)
⅓ cup well-drained sauerkraut
⅓ cup light or regular sour cream

1. Preheat broiler.

2. Melt butter in large skillet over medium-high heat. Separate onion slices into rings; add to skillet. Cook, stirring occasionally, until golden brown and tender, about 10 minutes.

3. Meanwhile, sprinkle 1 teaspoon paprika, garlic salt and pepper over both sides of pork chops. Place chops on rack of broiler pan.

4. Broil 4 to 5 inches from heat source 5 minutes. Turn; broil 4 to 5 minutes or until chops are barely pink in center.

5. Combine cooked onion with sauerkraut, sour cream and remaining ¼ teaspoon paprika; mix well. Garnish chops with onion mixture, or spread onion mixture over chops and return to broiler. Broil just until hot, about 1 minute.

Nutrients per Serving:
Calories: 216 (40% of calories from fat), Carbohydrate: 5g, Total Fat: 9g, Protein: 27g, Cholesterol: 83mg, Sodium: 420mg, Fiber: 1g

One Pan Pork Fu Yung

Makes 4 servings

- 1 cup fat-free reduced-sodium chicken broth
- ½ teaspoon dark sesame oil, divided
- 1 tablespoon cornstarch
- 2 teaspoons canola oil
- ½ pound boneless pork tenderloin, minced
- 1 cup sliced mushrooms
- 5 green onions, thinly sliced, divided
- ¼ teaspoon salt (optional)
- ¼ teaspoon white pepper
- 1 cup bean sprouts
- 2 eggs, well beaten
- 2 egg whites

1. Combine broth, ¼ teaspoon sesame oil and cornstarch in small pan. Cook, stirring occasionally, over medium heat until sauce thickens, about 5 to 6 minutes. Set aside.

2. Heat canola oil in 12-inch nonstick skillet over high heat. Add pork and stir-fry until no longer pink, about 4 minutes. Add remaining ¼ teaspoon sesame oil, mushrooms, all but 2 tablespoons of the green onions, salt, if desired, and pepper. Cook until lightly browned, 4 to 5 minutes.

3. Add sprouts and stir-fry, about 1 minute or less. With spatula, flatten pork mixture.

4. Mix eggs and egg whites; pour over pork mixture. Lower heat and cover pan. Cook until eggs are set, about 3 minutes.

5. To serve, cut into four pieces. Top each with ¼ cup sauce and remaining green onion.

Nutrients per Serving:
Calories: 189 (41% of calories from fat), Carbohydrate: 6g, Total Fat: 9g, Protein: 22g, Cholesterol: 149mg, Sodium: 150mg, Fiber: <1g

Roast Pork Chops with Apples and Cabbage

Makes 4 servings

3 teaspoons olive oil, divided
½ medium onion, thinly sliced
1 teaspoon dried thyme leaves
2 cloves garlic, minced
4 pork chops, 1 inch thick (6 to 8 ounces each)
¼ cup cider vinegar
1 tablespoon packed brown sugar
¼ teaspoon black pepper
1 large McIntosh apple, chopped
½ (8-ounce) package preshredded coleslaw mix

1. Heat 2 teaspoons oil in large skillet over medium-high heat until hot. Add onion. Cover; cook 4 to 6 minutes or until onion is tender, stirring often. Add thyme and garlic; stir 30 seconds. Transfer to small bowl; set aside.

2. Add remaining 1 teaspoon oil to skillet. Sprinkle pork chops with salt and pepper. Place in skillet; cook 2 minutes per side or until browned. Transfer pork chops to plate. Cover and refrigerate up to 1 day, if desired.

3. Remove skillet from heat. Add vinegar, sugar and pepper; stir to dissolve sugar and scrape cooked bits from skillet. Pour mixture into large bowl. Add onion mixture, apple and coleslaw mix; do not stir. Cover and refrigerate up to 1 day, if desired.

4. Preheat oven to 375°F. Place cabbage mixture in large ovenproof skillet. Heat over medium-high heat; stir until blended and liquid comes to a boil. Lay pork chops on top of cabbage mixture. Cover pan; place in oven. Bake 15 minutes or until pork chops are juicy and just barely pink in center.

Note: Instead of making ahead, prepare recipe through step 2 as directed above using ovenproof skillet, but do not refrigerate pork chops. Combine vinegar mixture, onion mixture, apple and cabbage in skillet; bring to a boil and top with pork chops. Complete recipe as directed.

Nutrients per Serving:
Calories: 241 (49% of calories from fat), Carbohydrate: 13g, Total Fat: 13g, Protein: 19g, Cholesterol: 60mg, Sodium: 66mg, Fiber: 1g

Roast Pork Chop with Apples and Cabbage

Zesty Skillet Pork Chops

Makes 4 servings

  1 teaspoon chili powder
½ teaspoon salt, divided
1¼ pounds lean pork chops, well trimmed of fat
  2 cups diced tomatoes
  1 cup chopped green, red or yellow bell pepper
¾ cup thinly sliced celery
½ cup chopped onion
  1 tablespoon hot pepper sauce
  1 teaspoon dried thyme leaves
    Nonstick cooking spray
  2 tablespoons finely chopped parsley

1. Rub chili powder and ¼ teaspoon salt evenly over one side of pork chops.

2. Combine tomatoes, bell pepper, celery, onion, pepper sauce and thyme in medium bowl; stir to blend.

3. Lightly coat 12-inch nonstick skillet with cooking spray. Heat over medium-high heat until hot. Add pork chops, seasoned side down; cook 1 minute. Turn pork; top with tomato mixture.

4. Bring to a boil. Reduce heat and simmer, covered, 25 minutes or until pork is tender and mixture has thickened.

5. Transfer pork to serving plates. Increase heat; bring tomato mixture to a boil and cook 2 minutes or until most of the liquid has evaporated. Remove from heat; stir in parsley and remaining ¼ teaspoon salt. Serve over pork.

Nutrients per Serving:
Calories: 172 (34% of calories from fat), Carbohydrate: 9g, Total Fat: 7g, Protein: 20g, Cholesterol: 49mg, Sodium: 387mg, Fiber: 3g

Peppered Pork Cutlets with Onion Gravy

Makes 4 servings

½ **teaspoon paprika**
¼ **teaspoon ground cumin**
¼ **teaspoon black pepper**
⅛ **teaspoon ground red pepper (optional)**
4 **boneless pork cutlets (4 ounces each), trimmed of fat**
   Nonstick cooking spray
2 **cups thinly sliced onion**
2 **tablespoons flour, divided**
¾ **cup water**
1½ **teaspoons chicken bouillon granules**
2 **tablespoons fat-free (skim) milk**
¼ **teaspoon salt**

1. Combine paprika, cumin, black pepper and red pepper, if desired; blend well. Sprinkle mixture evenly over one side of each cutlet and press down gently to adhere. Let stand 15 minutes to absorb flavors.

2. Heat large nonstick skillet over medium heat. Coat skillet with cooking spray. Add pork, seasoned side down, and cook 3 minutes or until browned. Remove from skillet and set aside on a plate, seasoned side up.

3. Increase heat to medium high. Coat skillet with cooking spray; add onions to pan and cook 4 minutes or until browned, stirring frequently. Sprinkle with 1½ tablespoons flour; toss to coat. Add water and bouillon; stir to blend and bring to a boil. Add cooked pork and any accumulated juices; spoon some of the sauce over pork. Reduce heat, cover and simmer 20 minutes or until pork is no longer pink in center.

4. Place pork on serving platter and set aside. Stir milk into onion mixture, or, for thicker consistency, blend together milk and ½ tablespoon flour and add to onion mixture. Add salt and cook 1 to 2 minutes. Spoon sauce over and around pork.

Nutrients per Serving:
Calories: 200 (27% of calories from fat), Carbohydrate: 7g, Total Fat: 6g, Protein: 26g, Cholesterol: 70mg, Sodium: 520mg, Fiber: <1g

Spicy Caribbean Pork Medallions

Makes 2 servings

6 ounces pork tenderloin
1 teaspoon Caribbean jerk seasoning
  Nonstick olive oil cooking spray
⅓ cup pineapple juice
1 teaspoon brown mustard
½ teaspoon cornstarch

1. Cut tenderloin into ½-inch-thick slices. Place each slice between 2 pieces of plastic wrap. Pound to ¼-inch thickness. Rub both sides of pork pieces with jerk seasoning.

2. Lightly spray large nonstick skillet with cooking spray; heat over medium heat until hot. Add pork. Cook 2 to 3 minutes or until no longer pink, turning once. Remove from skillet. Keep warm.

3. Stir together pineapple juice, mustard and cornstarch until smooth. Add to skillet. Cook and stir over medium heat until mixture comes to a boil and thickens slightly. Spoon over pork.

Nutrients per Serving:
Calories: 134 (23% of calories from fat), Carbohydrate: 7g, Total Fat: 3g, Protein: 18g, Cholesterol: 49mg, Sodium: 319mg, Fiber: <1g

Food Fact
Pork tenderloin is the tender strip of meat that lies along each side of the backbone. When it is cut crosswise into slices, it forms circles that are called medallions.

Pork Schnitzel

Makes 4 servings

    4 boneless pork chops, ¼ inch thick (3 ounces each)
    ½ cup cornflake crumbs or cracker crumbs
    1 egg, lightly beaten
       Black pepper
    2 to 4 teaspoons olive oil, divided
    ⅓ cup lemon juice
    ¼ cup chicken broth

1. Preheat oven to 200°F. Place ovenproof platter or baking sheet in oven. Trim fat from pork chops; discard fat. Place pork chops between layers of waxed paper; pound with smooth side of mallet to ⅛- to ¼-inch thickness. Place crumbs in medium bowl. Dip 1 pork chop at a time in egg; gently shake off excess. Dip in crumbs to coat both sides. Place breaded pork chops in single layer on plate. Sprinkle with pepper.

2. Heat 2 teaspoons oil in large skillet over medium-high heat until hot. Add pork chops in single layer. Cook 1 minute or until golden brown on bottom. Turn and cook ½ to 1 minute or until golden brown and no longer pink in center. Transfer to platter in oven. Repeat with remaining pork chops, adding oil as needed to prevent meat from sticking to skillet. Transfer to platter in oven.

3. Remove skillet from heat. Add lemon juice and broth. Stir to scrape cooked bits from pan bottom. Return to heat; bring to a boil, stirring constantly, until liquid is reduced to 3 to 4 tablespoons. Remove platter from oven. Pour lemon juice mixture over meat. Garnish as desired.

Nutrients per Serving:
Calories: 245 (44% of calories from fat), Carbohydrate: 13g, Total Fat: 12g, Protein: 21g, Cholesterol: 95mg, Sodium: 273mg, Fiber: 1g

Cuban Garlic & Lime Pork Chops

Makes 4 to 6 servings

6 boneless pork chops, ¾ inch thick (about 1½ pounds)
2 tablespoons olive oil
2 tablespoons lime juice
2 tablespoons orange juice
2 teaspoons minced garlic
½ teaspoon salt, divided
½ teaspoon red pepper flakes
2 small seedless oranges, peeled and chopped
1 medium cucumber, peeled, seeded and chopped
2 tablespoons chopped onion
2 tablespoons chopped fresh cilantro

1. Place pork in large resealable plastic food storage bag. Add oil, juices, garlic, ¼ teaspoon salt and red pepper flakes. Seal bag; turn to coat. Marinate in refrigerator up to 24 hours.

2. To make salsa, combine oranges, cucumber, onion and cilantro in small bowl; toss lightly. Cover and refrigerate 1 hour or overnight. Add remaining ¼ teaspoon salt just before serving.

3. Remove pork from marinade; discard marinade. Grill or broil pork 6 to 8 minutes on each side or until pork is no longer pink in center. Serve with salsa.

Nutrients per Serving:
Calories: 233 (46% of calories from fat), Carbohydrate: 11g, Total Fat: 12g, Protein: 20g, Cholesterol: 60mg, Sodium: 281mg, Fiber: 2g

Pork Curry Over Cauliflower Couscous

Makes 6 servings

> 3 tablespoons olive oil, divided
> 2 tablespoons mild curry powder
> 2 teaspoons prepared crushed garlic
> 1½ pounds pork (boneless shoulder, loin or chops), cubed
> 1 red or green bell pepper, seeded and diced
> 1 tablespoon cider vinegar
> ½ teaspoon salt
> 2 cups water
> 1 large head cauliflower

1. Heat 2 tablespoons oil in large saucepan over medium heat. Add curry powder and garlic; cook and stir 1 to 2 minutes until garlic is golden.

2. Add pork; stir to coat completely with curry and garlic. Cook and stir 5 to 7 minutes or until pork cubes are barely pink in center. Add bell pepper and vinegar; cook and stir 3 minutes or until bell pepper is soft. Sprinkle with salt.

3. Add water; bring to a boil. Reduce heat and simmer 30 to 45 minutes, stirring occasionally, until liquid is reduced and pork is tender, adding additional water as needed.

4. Meanwhile, trim and core cauliflower; cut into equal pieces. Place in food processor fitted with metal blade. Process using on/off pulsing action until cauliflower is in small uniform pieces about the size of cooked couscous. *Do not purée.*

5. Heat remaining 1 tablespoon oil in 12-inch nonstick skillet over medium heat. Add cauliflower; cook and stir 5 minutes or until crisp-tender. *Do not overcook.* Serve pork curry over cauliflower.

Nutrients per Serving:
Calories: 267 (51% of calories from fat), Carbohydrate: 7g, Total Fat: 15g, Protein: 28g, Cholesterol: 69mg, Sodium: 308mg, Fiber: 5g

Grilled Pork Tenderloin with Apple Salsa

Makes 4 servings

    1 tablespoon chili powder
    ½ teaspoon garlic powder
    1 pound pork tenderloin
    2 Granny Smith apples, peeled, cored and finely chopped
    1 can (4 ounces) chopped green chilies
    ¼ cup lemon juice
    3 tablespoons finely chopped fresh cilantro
    1 clove garlic, minced
    1 teaspoon dried oregano leaves, crushed
    ½ teaspoon salt

1. Spray grid well with nonstick cooking spray. Preheat grill to medium-high heat.

2. Combine chili powder and garlic powder in small bowl; mix well. Coat pork with spice mixture.

3. Grill pork 30 minutes, turning occasionally, until internal temperature reaches 165°F when tested with meat thermometer in thickest part of tenderloin. Transfer roast to cutting board; cover with foil. Let stand 10 to 15 minutes before slicing. Internal temperature will continue to rise 5°F to 10°F during stand time.

4. To make apple salsa, combine apples, chilies, lemon juice, cilantro, garlic, oregano and salt in medium bowl; mix well.

5. Slice pork across grain; serve with salsa. Garnish as desired.

Nutrients per Serving:
Calories: 201 (21% of calories from fat), Carbohydrate: 14g, Total Fat: 5g, Protein: 26g, Cholesterol: 81mg, Sodium: 678mg, Fiber: 2g

Roasted Pork in Pineapple-Chile Adobo

Makes 6 servings

 1 DOLE® Fresh Pineapple
 3 tablespoons packed brown sugar, divided
 1 to 2 tablespoons chopped canned chipotle peppers
 2 tablespoons lime juice
 1 tablespoon yellow mustard
 2 teaspoons dried oregano leaves, crushed
 ¼ teaspoon ground black pepper
 1½ pounds pork tenderloin
    Lime wedges

• Twist off crown from pineapple. Cut fresh pineapple in half lengthwise. Cut one half crosswise into about 1-inch thick slices. Cut remaining half in half. Refrigerate one quarter for another use. Core, skin and finely chop remaining quarter. Set aside.

• Arrange fresh pineapple slices in single layer on large baking sheet. Sprinkle with half of sugar. Set aside.

• Combine chopped fresh pineapple, peppers, lime juice, mustard, oregano and black pepper in shallow roasting pan. Add pork; spoon mixture over pork to cover all sides.

• Bake pork and pineapple at 400°F 40 to 50 minutes until pork is no longer pink in center and fresh pineapple is golden, turning pineapple halfway through cooking and sprinkling with remaining sugar. Let pork stand 5 minutes. Slice pork into ½-inch-thick slices. Serve with sugar-sprinkled pineapple and lime wedges.

Prep Time: 15 minutes
Bake Time: 50 minutes

Nutrients per Serving:
Calories: 245 (22% of calories from fat), Carbohydrate: 14g, Total Fat: 6g, Protein: 33g, Cholesterol: 105mg, Sodium: 133mg, Fiber: 4g

Smoky Mexican Pork Stir Fry

Makes 4 servings

- 1 small pork tenderloin (about 12 ounces)
- 4 slices bacon, diced
- 1 chipotle chile*
- 1 tablespoon vegetable oil
- 1 teaspoon ground cumin
- 1 teaspoon dried oregano
- 2 cloves garlic, crushed
- 1 red or green bell pepper, cut into thin strips
- 1 small onion, cut in half and thinly sliced
- 3 cups coarsely chopped romaine or iceberg lettuce

*If canned in adobo sauce, drain chile and chop; if dried, rehydrate in warm water, drain and chop.

Slice pork tenderloin in half lengthwise, then cut crosswise thinly. Toss pork, bacon and chipotle chile together in small bowl; set aside. Combine oil, cumin, oregano and garlic and heat in large nonstick skillet over medium-high heat. Add bell pepper and onion; stir-fry 2 to 3 minutes or until crisp-tender. Remove and reserve. In same skillet, stir-fry the pork, bacon and chile for 2 to 3 minutes until pork is just done and bacon crisp. Return vegetables to skillet and heat through. Serve over lettuce.

Favorite recipe from National Pork Board

Nutrients per Serving:
Calories: 199 (41% of calories from fat), Carbohydrate: 8g, Total Fat: 9g, Protein: 22g, Cholesterol: 62mg, Sodium: 186mg, Fiber: 2.5g

Maple-Mustard Pork Chops

Makes 2 servings

> 2 tablespoons maple syrup, divided
> 1 tablespoon olive oil
> 2 teaspoons whole-grain mustard
> 2 center-cut pork loin chops (6 ounces each)
>   Nonstick cooking spray
> ⅓ cup water

Preheat oven to 375°F. Combine maple syrup, olive oil and mustard in small bowl. Brush syrup mixture over both sides of pork chops. Spray medium ovenproof skillet with cooking spray; heat over medium-high heat. Add chops; brown on both sides. Add water; cover and bake 20 to 30 minutes or until barely pink in center.

Nutrients per Serving:
Calories: 286 (44% of calories from fat), Carbohydrate: 14g, Total Fat: 14g, Protein: 26g, Cholesterol: 70mg, Sodium: 102mg, Fiber: <1g

Salsa Chops

Makes 4 servings

> 4 pork chops, ¾-inch thick
>   Salt and pepper, to taste
> 1 teaspoon vegetable oil
> 1½ cups salsa

Season chops with salt and pepper. Heat oil in large nonstick skillet over medium-high heat and brown chops on one side, about 3 to 4 minutes. Turn chops and add salsa to skillet. Bring to a boil, lower heat, cover and simmer for 8 to 10 minutes.

Favorite recipe from National Pork Board

Nutrients per Serving:
Calories: 241 (56% of calories from fat), Carbohydrate: 2.5g, Total Fat: 14g, Protein: 23g, Cholesterol: 75mg, Sodium: 228mg, Fiber: <1g

Maple-Mustard Pork Chop

Tex-Mex Pork Kabobs with Chili Sour Cream Sauce

Makes 4 to 6 servings

2¼ teaspoons chili powder, divided
1¾ teaspoons cumin, divided
¾ teaspoon garlic powder, divided
¾ teaspoon onion powder, divided
¾ teaspoon oregano, divided
1 pork tenderloin (1½ pounds), trimmed and cut into 1-inch pieces
1 cup reduced-fat sour cream
¾ teaspoon salt, divided
¼ teaspoon black pepper
1 large red bell pepper, cored, seeded and cut into small chunks
1 large green bell pepper, cored, seeded and cut into small chunks
1 large yellow bell pepper, cored, seeded and cut into small chunks

1. Combine 1½ teaspoons chili powder, 1 teaspoon cumin, ½ teaspoon garlic powder, ½ teaspoon onion powder and ½ teaspoon oregano in medium bowl. Add pork. Toss to coat well. Cover tightly and refrigerate 2 to 3 hours.

2. Combine sour cream, remaining spices, ¼ teaspoon salt and pepper in small bowl. Mix well. Cover tightly and refrigerate 2 to 3 hours.

3. Preheat grill or broiler.

4. Toss pork with remaining ½ teaspoon salt. Thread meat and peppers onto skewers*. Grill over medium-hot coals 10 minutes until meat is no longer pink in center, turning several times. If broiling, place skewers on foil-lined baking sheet. Broil 8 inches from heat 5 minutes per side until no longer pink in center, turning once. Serve immediately with sour cream sauce.

*If using wooden skewers, soak in water 20 minutes before using.

Nutrients per Serving:
Calories: 320 (33% of calories from fat), Carbohydrate: 12g, Total Fat: 12g, Protein: 40g, Cholesterol: 119mg, Sodium: 564mg, Fiber: 2g

202

Grilled Pork Tenderloin Medallions

Makes 4 servings

Pepper & Herb Rub

    1 tablespoon garlic salt
    1 tablespoon dried basil leaves
    1 tablespoon dried thyme leaves
  1½ teaspoons cracked black pepper
  1½ teaspoons dried rosemary leaves
    1 teaspoon paprika

Pork

    2 tablespoons Pepper & Herb Rub
  12 pork tenderloin medallions (about 1 pound)
      Nonstick olive oil cooking spray

1. For rub, combine garlic salt, basil, thyme, pepper, rosemary and paprika in small jar or resealable plastic food storage bag. Store in cool dry place up to 3 months.

2. Prepare grill for direct cooking. Sprinkle rub evenly over both sides of pork, pressing lightly. Spray pork with cooking spray.

3. Place pork on grid over medium-hot coals. Grill, uncovered, 4 to 5 minutes per side or until no longer pink in center.

Nutrients per Serving:
Calories: 145 (27% of calories from fat), Carbohydrate: 2g, Total Fat: 4g, Protein: 24g, Cholesterol: 66mg, Sodium: 528mg, Fiber: 1g

Bolognese-Style Pork Ragú over Spaghetti Squash

Makes 8 servings

1½ pounds ground pork
1 cup finely chopped celery
½ cup chopped onion
1 teaspoon prepared crushed garlic *or* 2 cloves garlic, minced
2 tablespoons tomato paste
1 teaspoon Italian seasoning
1 can (14½ ounces) fat-free reduced-sodium chicken broth
½ cup half-and-half
1 spaghetti squash (3 to 4 pounds)
½ cup grated Parmesan cheese (optional)

1. Brown pork in 3-quart saucepan over medium-high heat, stirring to break up meat. Add celery and onion; cook and stir 5 minutes over medium heat or until vegetables are tender. Add garlic; cook and stir 1 minute. Stir in tomato paste and Italian seasoning.

2. Stir in broth. Reduce heat. Simmer 10 to 15 minutes, stirring occasionally.

3. Add half-and-half; cook and stir until hot. Skim off excess fat.

4. Meanwhile, pierce spaghetti squash several times with knife. Microwave at HIGH (100%) 15 minutes until squash is tender (squash will yield when pressed with finger). Let cool 10 to 15 minutes. Cut in half; scoop out and discard seeds. Separate flesh into strands with fork; keep squash warm.

5. Serve ½ cup meat sauce over 1 cup spaghetti squash. Sprinkle with 1 tablespoon grated Parmesan, if desired.

Tip: Sauce can be cooked the day before and refrigerated so that chilled fat can be easily removed and discarded before reheating.

Nutrients per Serving:
Calories: 333 (59% of calories from fat), Carbohydrate: 15g, Total Fat: 22g, Protein: 20g, Cholesterol: 75mg, Sodium: 275mg, Fiber: 2g

Simmering Fondue

Makes 4 servings

1 pound medium shrimp, peeled
8 ounces pork or beef tenderloin steaks, cut into thin slices
8 ounces lamb loin, cut into thin slices
2 cups sliced mushrooms
2 cups sliced carrots
2 cups broccoli florets
4 cans (14½ ounces each) fat-free reduced-sodium chicken broth
½ cup dry white wine
1 tablespoon chopped fresh parsley
1 teaspoon minced garlic
½ teaspoon dried thyme leaves
½ teaspoon dried rosemary

1. Arrange shrimp, pork, lamb, mushrooms, carrots and broccoli on large serving platter or in individual bowls.

2. Combine chicken broth, wine, parsley, garlic, thyme and rosemary in large saucepan. Bring to a boil over high heat. Remove from heat. Strain broth. Transfer broth to electric wok. Return to a simmer over high heat.

3. Thread any combination of shrimp, meat and vegetables onto bamboo skewers or fondue forks. Cook in broth 2 to 3 minutes.

Nutrients per Serving:
Calories: 324 (21% of calories from fat), Carbohydrate: 13g, Total Fat: 7g, Protein: 47g, Cholesterol: 219mg, Sodium: 1160mg, Fiber: 4g

Roasted Pork

Makes 4 servings

3 tablespoons barbecue sauce
1 tablespoon reduced-sodium soy sauce
1 tablespoon dry sherry
2 cloves garlic, minced
½ teaspoon crushed Szechwan peppercorns or red pepper flakes
2 whole pork tenderloins (about 1¼ to 1½ pounds total)

1. Preheat oven to 350°F. Combine barbecue sauce, soy sauce, sherry, garlic and peppercorns in small bowl.

2. Brush one-fourth of mixture evenly over each roast. Place roasts on rack in shallow foil-lined roasting pan. Cook roasts 15 minutes; turn and brush with remaining barbecue sauce mixture. Continue to cook until internal temperature reaches 165°F when tested with meat thermometer inserted in thickest part of roast. (Timing will depend on thickness of pork; test at 30 minutes.)

3. Transfer roast to cutting board; cover with foil. Let stand 10 to 15 minutes before carving. Internal temperature will continue to rise 5°F to 10°F. Slice diagonally and serve.

Nutrients per Serving:
Calories: 199 (26% of calories from fat), Carbohydrate: 3g, Total Fat: 5g, Protein: 32g, Cholesterol: 101mg, Sodium: 301mg, Fiber: <1g

Sherry Teriyaki Pork

Makes 4 servings

¼ cup plus 2 tablespoons light soy sauce
¼ cup sherry or apple juice (not cooking sherry)
2 tablespoons packed dark brown sugar
2 tablespoons cider vinegar
½ teaspoon red pepper flakes
1 pound pork tenderloin
   Black pepper
2 tablespoons diagonally sliced green onions

1. Combine soy sauce, sherry, sugar, vinegar and red pepper flakes in small bowl; stir until blended.

2. Place pork in shallow dish. Pour half the soy sauce mixture over pork; reserve remaining soy sauce mixture. Cover pork with plastic wrap; marinate in refrigerator 15 minutes, turning frequently. (Pork can be refrigerated and marinated overnight, if desired.)

3. Preheat oven to 425°F. Coat baking sheet with nonstick cooking spray. Remove pork from marinade; discard marinade. Place pork on prepared baking sheet and sprinkle heavily with black pepper. Bake 22 minutes or until slightly pink in center. Place pork on cutting board and let stand 5 minutes.

4. Meanwhile, place reserved soy sauce mixture in small skillet. Bring to a boil over high heat and continue to boil until reduced to ¼ cup, scraping bottom and sides of skillet frequently. Remove from heat.

5. Slice pork and arrange on platter. Drizzle with sauce and sprinkle with onions.

Nutrients per Serving:
Calories: 223 (25% of calories from fat), Carbohydrate: 12g, Total Fat: 6g, Protein: 26g, Cholesterol: 76mg, Sodium: 806mg, Fiber: <1g

Lemon-Capered Pork Tenderloin

Makes 8 servings

1 boneless pork tenderloin (about 1½ pounds)
1 tablespoon crushed capers
1 teaspoon dried rosemary leaves, crushed
⅛ teaspoon black pepper
1 cup water
¼ cup lemon juice

1. Preheat oven to 350°F. Trim fat from tenderloin; discard. Set tenderloin aside.

2. Combine capers, rosemary and black pepper in small bowl. Rub mixture over tenderloin. Place tenderloin in shallow roasting pan. Pour water and lemon juice over tenderloin.

3. Bake, uncovered, 1 hour or until thermometer inserted into thickest part of tenderloin registers 160°F. Remove from oven; cover with foil. Let stand 10 minutes. Cut evenly into 8 slices before serving. Garnish as desired.

Nutrients per Serving:
Calories: 114 (28% of calories from fat), Carbohydrate: <1g, Total Fat: 3g, Protein: 19g, Cholesterol: 45mg, Sodium: 59mg, Fiber: <1g

Food Fact

Capers are the flower buds of a bush native to the Mediterranean and parts of India. The buds are picked, sun-dried, then pickled. Capers should be rinsed before using to remove excess salt.

Garlic-Pepper Skewered Pork

Makes 4 to 6 servings (plus 6 chops for another meal)

> 1 boneless pork loin roast (about 2½ pounds)
> 6 to 15 cloves garlic, minced
> ⅓ cup lime juice
> 3 tablespoons firmly packed brown sugar
> 3 tablespoons soy sauce
> 2 tablespoons vegetable oil
> 2 teaspoons black pepper
> ¼ teaspoon cayenne pepper
> 8 green onions, cut into 2-inch pieces (optional)

Cut pork crosswise into six ½-inch-thick chops, reserving remaining roast. (Each chop may separate into 2 pieces.) Set chops aside in 13×9×2-inch glass dish. Cut remaining pork roast lengthwise into 2 pieces. Cut each piece into ⅛-inch-thick strips; place in dish with chops. To prepare marinade, combine all remaining ingredients except green onions in small bowl. Pour marinade over pork chops and slices; cover and refrigerate at least 1 hour or overnight. Thread pork slices ribbon style onto metal skewers, alternating pork with green onions. Grill skewered pork slices and chops over medium-hot KINGSFORD® Briquets about 3 minutes per side until no longer pink in center. (Chops may require 1 to 2 minutes longer.) *Do not overcook.* Serve skewered pork immediately. Cover and refrigerate chops for another convenient meal.

Nutrients per Serving:
Calories: 205 (37% of calories from fat), Carbohydrate: 6g, Total Fat: 8g, Protein: 25g, Cholesterol: 62mg, Sodium: 352mg, Fiber: <1g

Pork Medallions with Marsala

Makes 4 servings

1 pound pork tenderloin, cut into ½-inch slices
   All-purpose flour
2 tablespoons olive oil
1 clove garlic, minced
½ cup sweet marsala wine
2 tablespoons chopped fresh parsley

1. Lightly dust pork with flour. Heat oil in large skillet over medium-high heat until hot. Add pork slices; cook 3 minutes per side or until browned. Remove from pan. Reduce heat to medium.

2. Add garlic to skillet; cook and stir 1 minute. Add wine and pork; cook 3 minutes or until pork is barely pink in center. Remove pork from skillet. Stir in parsley. Simmer wine mixture until slightly thickened, 2 to 3 minutes. Serve over pork.

Nutrients per Serving:
Calories: 218 (45% of calories from fat), Carbohydrate: 1g, Total Fat: 11g, Protein: 24g, Cholesterol: 65mg, Sodium: 67mg, Fiber: <1g

Food Fact

Marsala is rich smoky-flavored wine imported from the Mediterranean island of Sicily. Sweet varietals are served with dessert or used for cooking while drier ones are served before meals.

Blackberry-Glazed Pork Medallions

Makes 4 servings

⅓ cup no-sugar-added seedless blackberry spread
4½ teaspoons red wine vinegar
1 tablespoon sugar
¼ teaspoon red pepper flakes
1 teaspoon vegetable oil
1 pound pork tenderloin, cut into ¼-inch slices
¼ teaspoon dried thyme leaves, divided
¼ teaspoon salt, divided

1. Whisk blackberry spread, vinegar, sugar and red pepper flakes in small bowl until blended; set aside.

2. Heat large nonstick skillet over medium-high heat until hot. Coat skillet with nonstick cooking spray; add oil and tilt skillet to coat bottom. Add half of pork slices; sprinkle with half of thyme and half of salt. Cook 2 minutes; turn and cook 1 minute on other side. Remove pork from skillet and set aside. Repeat with remaining pork, thyme and salt.

3. Add blackberry mixture to skillet; bring to a boil over high heat. Add reserved pork slices, discarding any accumulated juices. Cook about 4 minutes, turning constantly, until pork is richly glazed.

Nutrients per Serving:
Calories: 186 (26% of calories from fat), Carbohydrate: 10g, Total Fat: 5g, Protein: 23g, Cholesterol: 66mg, Sodium: 219mg, Fiber: <1g

Pork Tenderloin with Sherry-Mushroom Sauce

Makes 4 servings

1 lean pork tenderloin (1 to 1½ pounds)
1½ cups chopped button mushrooms or shiitake mushroom caps
2 tablespoons sliced green onion
1 clove garlic, minced
1 tablespoon reduced-fat margarine
1 tablespoon cornstarch
1 tablespoon chopped fresh parsley
½ teaspoon dried thyme leaves
Dash black pepper
⅓ cup water
1 tablespoon dry sherry
½ teaspoon beef bouillon granules

1. Preheat oven to 375°F. Place pork on rack in shallow baking pan. Insert meat thermometer into thickest part of tenderloin. Roast, uncovered, 25 to 35 minutes or until thermometer registers 165°F. Let stand, covered, 5 to 10 minutes while preparing sauce.

2. Cook and stir mushrooms, green onion and garlic in margarine in small saucepan over medium heat until vegetables are tender. Stir in cornstarch, parsley, thyme and pepper. Stir in water, sherry and bouillon granules. Cook and stir until sauce boils and thickens. Cook and stir 2 minutes more. Slice pork; serve with sauce.

Nutrients per Serving:
Calories: 179 (30% of calories from fat), Carbohydrate: 4g, Total Fat: 6g, Protein: 26g, Cholesterol: 81mg, Sodium: 205mg, Fiber: <1g

Caribbean Roast Pork

Makes 12 servings

1 (3-pound) pork loin roast
1 tablespoon black pepper
2 teaspoons olive oil
1 teaspoon nutmeg
1 teaspoon cinnamon

Blend pepper, oil, nutmeg and cinnamon in small bowl. Brush mixture evenly onto roast. Place pork in shallow pan; roast in 350°F oven for 1 to 1½ hours or until internal temperature is 155°F. Remove pork from oven; let stand 10 minutes before slicing.

Favorite recipe from National Pork Board

Nutrients per Serving:
Calories: 203 (37% of calories from fat), Carbohydrate: <1g, Total Fat: 8g, Protein: 30g, Cholesterol: 74mg, Sodium: 62mg, Fiber: <1g

Roasted Peppered Pork Tenderloin

Makes 8 servings

Boneless single loin pork roast, about 2 pounds
1 teaspoon garlic pepper spice blend
1 teaspoon dried rosemary, crushed

Heat oven to 350°F. Coat roast with garlic-pepper and rosemary; place in shallow roasting pan and roast for 45 minutes, until meat thermometer inserted reads 150 to 155°F. Remove from oven and let rest for 5 to 10 minutes before slicing to serve.

Favorite recipe from National Pork Board

Nutrients per Serving:
Calories: 126 (29% of calories from fat), Carbohydrate: <1g, Total Fat: 4g, Protein: 21g, Cholesterol: 63mg, Sodium: 161mg, Fiber: <1g

Peanut Pork Tenderloin

Makes 4 to 6 servings

⅓ **cup chunky unsweetened peanut butter**
⅓ **cup regular or light canned coconut milk**
¼ **cup lemon juice or dry white wine**
3 **tablespoons soy sauce**
3 **cloves garlic, minced**
2 **tablespoons sugar**
1 **piece (1-inch cube) fresh ginger, minced**
½ **teaspoon salt**
¼ **to ½ teaspoon cayenne pepper**
¼ **teaspoon ground cinnamon**
1½ **pounds pork tenderloin**

Combine peanut butter, coconut milk, lemon juice, soy sauce, garlic, sugar, ginger, salt, cayenne pepper and cinnamon in 2-quart glass dish until blended. Add pork; turn to coat. Cover and refrigerate at least 30 minutes or overnight. Remove pork from marinade; discard marinade. Grill pork on covered grill over medium KINGSFORD® Briquets about 20 minutes until just barely pink in center, turning 4 times. Cut crosswise into ½-inch slices. Serve immediately.

Nutrients per Serving:
Calories: 248 (29% of calories from fat), Carbohydrate: 2g, Total Fat: 8g, Protein: 39g, Cholesterol: 125mg, Sodium: 217mg, Fiber: 2g

Food Fact

Coconut milk and a richer coconut cream may be purchased in Asian markets or specialty food stores. They may also be prepared at home. Used in many tropical and Asian dishes, coconut milk and cream add flavor to curries, puddings and sauces. Coconut milk should not be confused with the thin liquid that may be drained from a fresh coconut before the meat is removed.

Snacks

Polenta Triangles

Makes 8 servings

½ **cup yellow corn grits**
1½ **cups fat-free reduced-sodium chicken broth, divided**
2 **cloves garlic, minced**
½ **cup (2 ounces) crumbled feta cheese**
1 **red bell pepper, roasted,* peeled and finely chopped**

*Place pepper on foil-lined broiler pan; broil 15 minutes or until blackened on all sides, turning every 5 minutes. Place pepper in paper bag; close bag and let stand 15 minutes before peeling.

1. Combine grits and ½ cup chicken broth in small bowl; mix well and set aside. Pour remaining 1 cup broth into large heavy saucepan; bring to a boil. Add garlic and moistened grits; mix well and return to a boil. Reduce heat to low; cover and cook 20 minutes. Remove from heat; add feta cheese. Stir until cheese is completely melted. Add roasted bell pepper; mix well.

2. Spray 8-inch square pan with nonstick cooking spray. Spoon grits mixture into prepared pan. Press grits evenly into pan with wet fingertips. Refrigerate until cold.

3. Spray grid with nonstick cooking spray. Prepare grill for direct cooking. Turn polenta out onto cutting board and cut into 2-inch squares. Cut each square diagonally into 2 triangles.

4. Place polenta triangles on grid. Grill over medium-high heat 1 minute or until bottoms are lightly browned. Turn triangles over and grill until browned and crisp. Serve warm or at room temperature.

Nutrients per Serving:
Calories: 62 (26% of calories from fat), Carbohydrate: 9g, Total Fat: 2g, Protein: 3g, Cholesterol: 6mg, Sodium: 142mg, Fiber: <1g

Cranberry Salad

Makes 8 servings

2 cups cranberries
1 cup water
1 cup EQUAL® SPOONFUL*
1 small package cranberry or cherry sugar-free gelatin
1 cup boiling water
1 cup diced celery
1 can (7¼ ounces) crushed pineapple, in juice
½ cup chopped walnuts

*May substitute 24 packets Equal® sweetener.

• Bring cranberries and 1 cup water to a boil. Remove from heat when cranberries have popped open. Add Equal® and stir. Set aside to cool.

• Dissolve gelatin with 1 cup boiling water. Add cranberry sauce; mix thoroughly. Add celery, pineapple and walnuts. Pour into mold or bowl. Place in refrigerator until set.

Nutrients per Serving:
Calories: 96 (47% of calories from fat), Carbohydrate: 11g, Total Fat: 5g, Protein: 2g, Cholesterol: 0mg, Sodium: 49mg, Fiber: 2g

Food Fact

Cranberries are native to North America. Pilgrims noticed that the cranes flew to the cranberry bogs in great flocks and feasted on the sour red berries. Thus they got their name--not craneberries but cranberries.

Jalapeño Wild Rice Cakes

Makes 8 (3-inch diameter) rice cakes

¾ **cup water**
⅓ **cup wild rice**
½ **teaspoon salt, divided**
1 **tablespoon all-purpose flour**
½ **teaspoon baking powder**
1 **egg**
1 **jalapeño pepper,* finely chopped**
2 **tablespoons minced onion**
1 **tablespoon freshly grated ginger** *or* **2 teaspoons ground ginger**
2 **tablespoons vegetable or olive oil**

*Jalapeño peppers can sting and irritate the skin; wear rubber gloves when handling peppers and do not touch eyes. Wash hands after handling.

1. Combine water, rice and ¼ teaspoon salt in medium saucepan. Bring to a boil. Reduce heat; cover and simmer 40 to 45 minutes or until rice is tender. Drain rice, if necessary; place in medium bowl. Add flour, baking powder and remaining ¼ teaspoon salt; mix until blended.

2. Whisk egg, jalapeño pepper, onion and ginger together in small bowl. Pour egg mixture over rice; mix until well blended.

3. Heat oil in large nonstick skillet over medium heat. Shape 2 tablespoons rice mixture into patties and place in pan. Cook, 4 cakes at a time, 3 minutes on each side or until golden brown. Transfer to paper towels. Serve immediately or refrigerate up to 24 hours.

Tip: To reheat cold rice cakes, preheat oven to 400°F. Place rice cakes in single layer on baking sheet; heat 5 minutes.

Nutrients per Serving:
Calories: 63 (57% of calories from fat), Carbohydrate: 5g, Total Fat: 4g, Protein: 2g, Cholesterol: 27mg, Sodium: 330mg, Fiber: <1g

Finger Licking Chicken Salad

Makes 1 serving

½ **cup diced roasted skinless chicken breast**
½ **rib celery, cut into 1-inch pieces**
¼ **cup drained mandarin orange segments**
¼ **cup red seedless grapes**
2 **tablespoons fat-free, sugar-free lemon yogurt**
1 **tablespoon reduced-fat mayonnaise**
¼ **teaspoon reduced-sodium soy sauce**
⅛ **teaspoon pumpkin pie spice or cinnamon**

1. Toss together chicken, celery, oranges and grapes in plastic container; cover.

2. For dipping sauce, combine yogurt, mayonnaise, soy sauce and pumpkin pie spice in small bowl. Place in small plastic container; cover.

3. Pack chicken mixture and dipping sauce in insulated bag with ice pack. To serve, dip chicken mixture into dipping sauce.

Serving Suggestion: Thread the chicken on wooden skewers alternately with celery, oranges and grapes.

Nutrients per Serving:
Calories: 207 (25% of calories from fat), Carbohydrate: 15g, Total Fat: 6g, Protein: 24g, Cholesterol: 64mg, Sodium: 212mg, Fiber: 1g

Turkey-Ham Quesadillas

Makes 8 appetizer servings

¼ **cup picante sauce or salsa**
 4 **(7-inch) regular or whole wheat flour tortillas**
½ **cup shredded reduced-fat reduced-sodium Monterey Jack cheese**
¼ **cup finely chopped turkey-ham or lean ham**
¼ **cup canned diced green chilies, drained** *or* **1 to 2 tablespoons chopped jalapeño**
    peppers*
Nonstick cooking spray
Additional picante sauce or salsa for dipping (optional)
Fat-free or reduced-fat sour cream (optional)

*Jalapeño peppers can sting and irritate the skin; wear rubber gloves when handling peppers and do not touch eyes. Wash hands after handling.

1. Spread 1 tablespoon picante sauce on each tortilla.

2. Sprinkle cheese, turkey-ham and chilies equally over half of each tortilla. Fold over uncovered half to make quesadilla; spray tops and bottoms of quesadillas with cooking spray.

3. Grill on uncovered grill over medium coals 1½ minutes per side or until cheese is melted and tortillas are golden brown, turning once. Quarter each quesadilla and serve with additional picante sauce and fat-free sour cream, if desired.

Nutrients per Serving:
Calories: 82 (24% of calories from fat), Carbohydrate: 11g, Total Fat: 2g, Protein: 5g, Cholesterol: 5mg, Sodium: 226mg, Fiber: 1g

Herbed Potato Chips

Makes 6 servings (about 60 chips)

    Nonstick olive oil cooking spray
2 medium red potatoes (about ½ pound), unpeeled
1 tablespoon olive oil
2 tablespoons minced fresh dill, thyme or rosemary *or* 2 teaspoons dried dill weed,
    thyme or rosemary
¼ teaspoon garlic salt
⅛ teaspoon black pepper
1¼ cups fat-free sour cream

1. Preheat oven to 450°F. Spray large baking sheets with cooking spray; set aside.

2. Cut potatoes crosswise into very thin slices, about 1/16 inch thick. Pat dry with paper towels. Arrange potato slices in single layer on prepared baking sheets; coat potatoes with cooking spray.

3. Bake 10 minutes; turn slices over. Brush with oil. Combine dill, garlic salt and pepper in small bowl; sprinkle evenly onto potato slices. Continue baking 5 to 10 minutes or until potatoes are golden brown. Cool on baking sheets.

4. Serve with sour cream.

Nutrients per Serving:
Calories: 76 (26% of calories from fat), Carbohydrate: 9g, Total Fat: 2g, Protein: 6g, Cholesterol: 0mg, Sodium: 113mg, Fiber: <1g

Tabbouleh

Makes 8 servings

½ cup uncooked bulgur wheat
¾ cup boiling water
¼ teaspoon salt
1 tablespoon plus 2 teaspoons lemon juice
2 teaspoons olive oil
½ teaspoon dried basil leaves
¼ teaspoon black pepper
1 green onion, thinly sliced
½ cup chopped cucumber
½ cup chopped green bell pepper
½ cup chopped tomato
¼ cup chopped fresh parsley
2 teaspoons chopped mint (optional)

1. Rinse bulgur thoroughly in colander under cold water, picking out any debris; drain well. Transfer to medium heatproof bowl. Stir in boiling water and salt. Cover; let stand 30 minutes. Drain well.

2. Combine lemon juice, oil, basil and black pepper in small bowl. Pour over bulgur; mix well.

3. Layer bulgur, onion, cucumber, bell pepper and tomato in clear glass bowl; sprinkle with parsley and mint, if desired.

4. Refrigerate, covered, at least 2 hours to allow flavors to blend. Serve layered or toss before serving.

Nutrients per Serving:
Calories: 49 (23% of calories from fat), Carbohydrate: 9g, Total Fat: 1g, Protein: 1g, Cholesterol: 0mg, Sodium: 71mg, Fiber: 3g

Peaches and Creamy Dip with Waffle Wedges

Makes 24 wedges and about ¾ cup cream cheese mixture

4 ounces reduced-fat cream cheese
⅓ cup no-sugar-added peach preserves
1 tablespoon fat-free (skim) milk
2 packets sugar substitute
½ teaspoon vanilla
4 low-fat toaster waffles
Ground cinnamon

1. Place all ingredients except waffles and cinnamon in blender and process until smooth. Set aside.

2. Toast waffles and cut each into 6 wedges.

3. Place cream cheese mixture in small serving bowl and sprinkle with cinnamon. Serve with waffle wedges for dipping.

Nutrients per Serving:
Calories: 54 (29% of calories from fat), Carbohydrate: 5g, Total Fat: 3g, Protein: 2g, Cholesterol: <1mg, Sodium: 57mg, Fiber: <1g

Food Fact

Cream cheese is an American original that was developed over a century ago. It was first produced commercially by a farmer in upstate New York and used as a spread on breads, crackers and bagels.

Spiced Sesame Wonton Crisps

Makes 8 servings

20 (3-inch-square) wonton wrappers, cut in half
 1 tablespoon water
 2 teaspoons olive oil
½ teaspoon paprika
½ teaspoon ground cumin or chili powder
¼ teaspoon dry mustard
 1 tablespoon sesame seeds

1. Preheat oven to 375°F. Coat 2 large nonstick baking sheets with nonstick cooking spray.

2. Cut each halved wonton wrapper into 2 strips; place in single layer on prepared baking sheets.

3. Combine water, oil, paprika, cumin and mustard in small bowl; mix well. Brush oil mixture evenly onto wonton strips; sprinkle evenly with sesame seeds.

4. Bake 6 to 8 minutes or until lightly browned. Remove to wire rack; cool completely. Transfer to serving plate.

Nutrients per Serving:
Calories: 75 (24% of calories from fat), Carbohydrate: 12g, Total Fat: 2g, Protein: 2g, Cholesterol: 3mg, Sodium: 116mg, Fiber: <1g

Sparkling Strawberry-Lime Shake

Makes 2 servings

 2 cups (10 ounces) frozen whole unsweetened strawberries
1¼ cups lime-flavored sparkling water, divided
 ¼ cup whipping cream or half-and-half
 1 tablespoon sugar substitute
    Lime wedges or slices

1. Place strawberries in blender container; let thaw 5 minutes before proceeding.
Add 1 cup sparkling water, cream and sugar substitute. Cover; blend until smooth, scraping down side of blender once or twice (mixture will be thick).

2. Gently stir in remaining sparkling water; pour into 2 glasses. Garnish with lime wedges.

Variation: For a tropical variation, add 1 teaspoon banana extract and/or ½ teaspoon coconut extract along with the cream.

Tip: For quick shakes anytime, wash, hull and freeze whole strawberries in a tightly covered container.

Nutrients per Serving:
Calories: 156 (70% of calories from fat), Carbohydrate: 15g, Total Fat: 12g, Protein: 2g, Cholesterol: 41mg, Sodium: 18mg, Fiber: 2g

Rosemary Breadsticks

Makes 12 servings (12 breadsticks)

⅔ cup reduced-fat (2%) milk
¼ cup finely chopped fresh chives
 2 teaspoons baking powder
 1 teaspoon finely chopped fresh rosemary *or* ½ teaspoon dried rosemary leaves
¾ teaspoon salt
½ teaspoon black pepper
¾ cup whole wheat flour
¾ cup all-purpose flour
   Nonstick cooking spray

1. Combine milk, chives, baking powder, rosemary, salt and pepper in large bowl; mix well. Stir in flours, ½ cup at a time, until blended. Turn onto floured surface and knead dough about 5 minutes or until smooth and elastic, adding more flour if dough is sticky. Let stand 30 minutes at room temperature.

2. Preheat oven to 375°F. Spray baking sheet with cooking spray. Divide dough into 12 balls. Roll each ball into long thin rope; place on prepared baking sheet. Lightly spray breadsticks with cooking spray. Bake about 12 minutes or until bottoms are golden brown. Turn breadsticks over; bake about 10 minutes more or until golden brown.

Nutrients per Serving:
Calories: 62 (7% of calories from fat), Carbohydrate: 12g, Total Fat: 1g, Protein: 2g, Cholesterol: 1mg, Sodium: 196mg, Fiber: 1g

Monterey Wedges

Makes 4 servings (2 wedges each)

2 (6-inch) corn tortillas
¼ cup (1 ounce) shredded reduced-fat Monterey Jack or sharp Cheddar cheese
½ teaspoon chili powder
½ cup chopped green bell pepper
1 plum tomato, chopped (about ¼ cup)
¼ cup sliced ripe olives, drained
2 tablespoons chopped canned green chilies

1. Preheat oven 425°F. Coat nonstick baking sheet with nonstick cooking spray.

2. Place tortillas on baking sheet; top each with 2 tablespoons cheese, half the chili powder, bell pepper, tomato, olives and chilies. Top with remaining 2 tablespoons cheese.

3. Bake 5 minutes or until cheese melts. Remove from oven and let stand on baking sheet 3 minutes for easier handling. Cut into 4 wedges.

Nutrients per Serving:
Calories: 85 (47% of calories from fat), Carbohydrate: 8g, Total Fat: 5g, Protein: 3g, Cholesterol: 5mg, Sodium: 387mg, Fiber: 1g

Portobello Mushrooms Sesame

Makes 4 servings

> 2 tablespoons sweet rice wine
> 2 tablespoons reduced-sodium soy sauce
> 2 cloves garlic, minced
> 1 teaspoon dark sesame oil
> 4 large portobello mushrooms, stemmed

Combine wine, soy sauce, garlic and oil in small bowl. Brush both sides of mushroom caps with soy sauce mixture. Grill mushrooms, top side up, on covered grill over medium coals 3 to 4 minutes. Brush tops with soy sauce mixture and turn over; grill 2 minutes more or until mushrooms are lightly browned. Turn again and grill, basting frequently, 4 to 5 minutes or until tender when pressed with back of spatula. Remove mushrooms and cut diagonally into ½-inch-thick slices.

Nutrients per Serving:
Calories: 67 (21% of calories from fat), Carbohydrate: 9g, Total Fat: 2g, Protein: 4g, Cholesterol: 0mg, Sodium: 268mg, Fiber: <1g

Fast Guacamole and "Chips"

Makes 8 servings, about 1¾ cups

> 2 ripe avocados
> ½ cup chunky salsa
> ¼ teaspoon hot pepper sauce (optional)
> ½ seedless cucumber, sliced into ⅛-inch rounds

Cut avocados in half; remove and discard pits. Scoop flesh into medium bowl. Mash with fork. Add salsa and pepper sauce, if desired; mix well. Transfer guacamole to serving bowl; surround with cucumber "chips".

Nutrients per Serving:
Calories: 85 (72% of calories from fat), Carbohydrate: 5g, Total Fat: 7g, Protein: 2g, Cholesterol: 0mg, Sodium: 120mg, Fiber: 2g

Taco Popcorn Olé

Makes 6 (1½-cup) servings

9 cups air-popped popcorn
   Butter-flavored cooking spray
1 teaspoon chili powder
½ teaspoon salt
½ teaspoon garlic powder
⅛ teaspoon ground red pepper (optional)

1. Preheat oven to 350°F. Line 15×10-inch jelly-roll pan with foil.

2. Place popcorn in single layer in prepared pan. Coat lightly with cooking spray.

3. Combine chili powder, salt, garlic powder and red pepper, if desired, in small bowl; sprinkle over popcorn. Mix lightly to coat evenly.

4. Bake 5 minutes or until hot, stirring gently after 3 minutes. Spread mixture in single layer on large sheet of foil to cool.

Tip: Store popcorn mixture in tightly covered container at room temperature up to 4 days.

Nutrients per Serving:
Calories: 48 (10% of calories from fat), Carbohydrate: 10g, Total Fat: 1g, Protein: 2g, Cholesterol: 0mg, Sodium: 199mg, Fiber: 2g

Southern Crab Cakes with Rémoulade Dipping Sauce

Makes 8 servings

10 ounces fresh lump crabmeat
1½ cups fresh white or sourdough bread crumbs, divided
¼ cup chopped green onions
½ cup fat-free or reduced-fat mayonnaise, divided
1 egg white, lightly beaten
2 tablespoons coarse grain or spicy brown mustard, divided
¾ teaspoon hot pepper sauce, divided
2 teaspoons olive oil, divided
Lemon wedges

1. Preheat oven to 200°F. Combine crabmeat, ¾ cup bread crumbs and green onions in medium bowl. Add ¼ cup mayonnaise, egg white, 1 tablespoon mustard and ½ teaspoon pepper sauce; mix well. Using ¼ cup mixture per cake, shape eight ½-inch-thick cakes. Roll crab cakes lightly in remaining ¾ cup bread crumbs.

2. Heat large nonstick skillet over medium heat until hot; add 1 teaspoon oil. Add 4 crab cakes; cook 4 to 5 minutes per side or until golden brown. Transfer to serving platter; keep warm in oven. Repeat with remaining 1 teaspoon oil and crab cakes.

3. To prepare dipping sauce, combine remaining ¼ cup mayonnaise, 1 tablespoon mustard and ¼ teaspoon hot pepper sauce in small bowl; mix well.

4. Serve crab cakes warm with lemon wedges and dipping sauce.

Nutrients per Serving:
Calories: 81 (25% of calories from fat), Carbohydrate: 8g, Total Fat: 2g, Protein: 7g, Cholesterol: 30mg, Sodium: 376mg, Fiber: <1g

Oriental Chicken Balls

Makes 10 servings (about 30 to 34 appetizers)

1 tablespoon butter or margarine
1 tablespoon all-purpose flour
½ cup warm milk
3 tablespoons finely chopped onion
1 cup chopped cooked chicken
1 teaspoon lemon juice
1 tablespoon chopped fresh parsley
½ teaspoon salt
⅛ teaspoon ground black pepper
⅓ cup cornstarch
   Vegetable oil for frying
   Sweet-and-sour sauce

Melt butter in small skillet over medium heat until hot; stir in flour and cook until smooth and lightly browned. Slowly stir in milk until sauce is thick and smooth. Bring to a boil, stirring constantly. Stir in onion; cook about 5 minutes over low heat. Stir in chicken, lemon juice, parsley, salt and pepper; transfer to small bowl. Refrigerate until cold. Shape into 1-inch balls; keep refrigerated until ready to cook. Place cornstarch on wax paper. Roll chicken balls in cornstarch. Heat 1 inch oil in large skillet to 375°F. Add chicken balls; cook only until light brown. Serve hot with sweet-and-sour sauce for dipping.

Favorite recipe from National Chicken Council

Nutrients per Serving:
Calories: 201 (72% of calories from fat), Carbohydrate: 10g, Total Fat: 16g, Protein: 4g, Cholesterol: 16mg, Sodium: 166mg, Fiber: 0g

Pineapple-Mango Salsa

Makes 3 ½ cups

1½ cups DOLE® Fresh Pineapple Chunks
1 ripe DOLE® Mango, peeled and chopped
½ cup chopped red cabbage
⅓ cup finely chopped DOLE® Red Onion
¼ cup chopped fresh cilantro
2 tablespoons lime juice
1 to 2 serrano or jalapeño chiles, seeded and minced

• Stir together pineapple chunks, mango, cabbage, red onion, cilantro, lime juice and chiles in medium bowl. Cover and chill for at least 30 minutes to blend flavors. Serve salsa over grilled chicken with grilled vegetables. Garnish with lime wedges, if desired.

• Salsa can also be served as a dip with tortilla chips or spooned over quesadillas or tacos.

Prep Time: 15 minutes
Chill Time: 30 minutes

Nutrients per Serving:
Calories: 10 (5% of calories from fat), Carbohydrate: 3g, Total Fat: <1g, Protein: <1g, Cholesterol: 0mg, Sodium: <1mg, Fiber: <1g

Food Fact

Varying in size, shape and color, the yellowish orange flesh of the mango has a rich flavor and a spicy aroma. Mangoes must be fully ripe before eating or using in recipes. Allow them to ripen at room temperature until soft, then use or refrigerate for a few days.

Mexican Roll-Ups

Makes 12 appetizers

 6 uncooked lasagna noodles
¾ cup prepared guacamole
¾ cup chunky salsa
¾ cup (3 ounces) shredded fat-free Cheddar cheese
    Additional salsa (optional)

1. Cook lasagna noodles according to package directions, omitting salt. Rinse with cool water; drain. Cool.

2. Spread 2 tablespoons guacamole onto each noodle; top each with 2 tablespoons salsa and 2 tablespoons cheese.

3. Roll up noodles jelly-roll fashion. Cut each roll-up in half to form two equal-size roll-ups. Serve immediately with additional salsa, if desired, or cover with plastic wrap and refrigerate up to 3 hours.

Nutrients per Serving:
Calories: 40 (28% of calories from fat), Carbohydrate: 4g, Total Fat: 1g, Protein: 3g, Cholesterol: 2mg, Sodium: 218mg, Fiber: 1g

Savory Zucchini Sticks

Makes 4 servings

    Nonstick olive oil cooking spray
3 tablespoons seasoned dry bread crumbs
2 tablespoons grated Parmesan cheese
1 egg white
1 teaspoon reduced-fat (2%) milk
2 small zucchini (about 4 ounces each), cut lengthwise into quarters
⅓ cup spaghetti sauce, warmed

1. Preheat oven to 400°F. Spray baking sheet with cooking spray; set aside.

2. Combine bread crumbs and Parmesan cheese in shallow dish. Combine egg white and milk in another shallow dish; beat with fork until well blended.

3. Dip each zucchini wedge first into crumb mixture, then into egg white mixture, letting excess drip back into dish. Roll again in crumb mixture to coat.

4. Place zucchini sticks on prepared baking sheet; coat well with cooking spray. Bake 15 to 18 minutes or until golden brown. Serve with spaghetti sauce.

Nutrients per Serving:
Calories: 69 (26% of calories from fat), Carbohydrate: 9g, Total Fat: 2g, Protein: 4g, Cholesterol: 6mg, Sodium: 329mg, Fiber: 1g

Szechuan Chicken Tenders

Makes 4 servings

   2 **tablespoons soy sauce**
   1 **tablespoon chili sauce**
   1 **tablespoon dry sherry**
   2 **cloves garlic, minced**
 ¼ **teaspoon red pepper flakes**
 16 **chicken tenders (about 1 pound)**
   1 **tablespoon peanut oil**
     Hot cooked rice (optional)

1. Combine soy sauce, chili sauce, sherry, garlic and red pepper flakes in shallow dish. Add chicken; coat well.

2. Heat oil in large nonstick skillet over medium heat until hot. Add chicken; cook 6 minutes, turning once, until chicken is browned and no longer pink in center.

3. Serve chicken with rice, if desired.

Tip: If you can "take the heat," try adding a few Szechuan peppers to the dish. They are best if heated in the oven or over a low flame in a skillet for a few minutes before serving.

Nutrients per Serving:
Calories: 180 (30% of calories from fat), Carbohydrate: 3g, Total Fat: 6g, Protein: 26g, Cholesterol: 69mg, Sodium: 625mg, Fiber: <1g

Curly Lettuce Wrappers

Makes 4 servings

4 green leaf lettuce leaves
¼ cup reduced-fat sour cream
4 turkey bacon slices, crisp-cooked and crumbled
½ cup (2 ounces) crumbled feta or blue cheese
8 ounces thinly sliced deli turkey breast
4 whole green onions
½ medium red or green bell pepper, thinly sliced
1 cup broccoli sprouts

1. Rinse lettuce leaves and pat dry.

2. Combine sour cream and bacon in small bowl. Spread ¼ of sour cream mixture evenly over center third of one lettuce leaf. Sprinkle 2 tablespoons cheese over sour cream. Top with 2 ounces turkey.

3. Cut off green portion of each green onion, reserving white onion bottoms for another use. Place green portion of 1 onion, ¼ of bell pepper slices and ¼ cup sprouts on top of turkey.

4. Fold right edge of lettuce over filling; fold bottom edge up over filling. Loosely roll up from folded right edge, leaving left edge of wrap open. Repeat with remaining ingredients.

Travel Tip: Wrap individually in plastic wrap. Store in cooler with ice.

Nutrients per Serving:
Calories: 155 (41% of calories from fat), Carbohydrate: 6g, Total Fat: 7g, Protein: 17g, Cholesterol: 75mg, Sodium: 987mg, Fiber: <1g

Wild Wedges

Makes 4 servings

> 2 (8-inch) fat-free flour tortillas
>   Nonstick cooking spray
> ⅓ cup shredded reduced-fat Cheddar cheese
> ⅓ cup chopped cooked chicken or turkey
> 1 green onion, thinly sliced
> 2 tablespoons mild, thick and chunky salsa

1. Heat large nonstick skillet over medium heat until hot.

2. Spray one side of one flour tortilla with cooking spray; place in skillet sprayed side down. Top with cheese, chicken, green onion and salsa. Place remaining tortilla over mixture; spray with cooking spray.

3. Cook 2 to 3 minutes per side or until golden brown and cheese is melted. Cut into 8 triangles.

Variation: For bean quesadillas, omit the chicken and spread ⅓ cup canned fat-free refried beans over one of the tortillas.

Nutrients per Serving:
Calories: 76 (24% of calories from fat), Carbohydrate: 8g, Total Fat: 2g, Protein: 7g, Cholesterol: 14mg, Sodium: 282mg, Fiber: 4g

Hot or Cold Tuna Snacks

Makes 6 servings

4 ounces light cream cheese
1 can (6 ounces) water-packed chunk light tuna, well drained
1 tablespoon chopped fresh parsley
1 tablespoon minced onion
½ teaspoon oregano
½ teaspoon pepper
18 (½-inch) thick slices of seedless cucumber
18 capers for garnish, optional

1. Combine cream cheese, tuna, parsley, onion, oregano and pepper in medium bowl; mix well.

2. Mound about 1 tablespoon of the tuna mixture to completely cover top of each cucumber slice, using the inside edge of a teaspoon to shape mixture. If serving cold, garnish each with a caper, if desired.

3. To serve hot, preheat oven to 500°F. Spray a baking sheet with cooking spray. Place on prepared baking sheet and bake until tops are puffed and brown, about 10 minutes.

4. Remove from oven and transfer to serving plate.

Nutrients per Serving:
Calories: 83 (44% of calories from fat), Carbohydrate: 2g, Total Fat: 5g, Protein: 9g, Cholesterol: 21mg, Sodium: 196mg, Fiber: <1g

Red Hot Pepper Wings

Makes 7 servings

28 chicken wing drumettes (2¼ to 3 pounds)
2 tablespoons olive oil
  Salt and black pepper
2 tablespoons melted butter
1 teaspoon sugar
¼ to ½ cup hot pepper sauce

Brush chicken with oil; sprinkle with salt and pepper. Grill chicken on covered grill over medium KINGSFORD® Briquets about 20 minutes until juices run clear, turning every 5 minutes. Combine butter, sugar and pepper sauce in large bowl; add chicken and toss to coat. Serve hot or cold.

Nutrients per Serving:
Calories: 495 (70% of calories from fat), Carbohydrate: <1g, Total Fat: 38g, Protein: 36g, Cholesterol: 159mg, Sodium: 194mg, Fiber: <1g

Cranberry-Lime Party Punch

Makes 10 (8 ounce) servings

7½ cups low-calorie cranberry juice cocktail
½ cup fresh lime juice
6 packets sugar substitute *or* equivalent of ¼ cup sugar
2 cups ice cubes
1 cup sugar-free ginger ale or sugar-free lemon-lime soda
1 lime, sliced
  Fresh cranberries for garnish (optional)

Combine cranberry juice, lime juice and sugar substitute in punch bowl; stir until sugar substitute dissolves.

Stir in ice cubes, ginger ale and lime slices; garnish with fresh cranberries, if desired.

Nutrients per Serving:
Calories: 38 (0% of calories from fat), Carbohydrate: 9g, Total Fat: 0g, Protein: <1g, Cholesterol: 0mg, Sodium: 61mg, Fiber: 0g

Desserts

Chocolate Peanut Butter Ice Cream Sandwiches

Makes 4 servings

> 2 tablespoons creamy peanut butter
> 8 chocolate wafer cookies
> ⅔ cup no-sugar-added vanilla ice cream, softened

1. Spread peanut butter evenly over flat sides of all cookies.

2. Spoon about 2½ tablespoons ice cream over peanut butter on 4 cookies. Top with remaining 4 cookies, peanut butter sides down. Press down lightly to force ice cream to edges of sandwich.

3. Wrap each sandwich in foil; seal tightly. Freeze at least 2 hours or up to 5 days.

Nutrients per Serving:
Calories: 129 (49% of calories from fat), Carbohydrate: 15g, Total Fat: 7g, Protein: 4g, Cholesterol: 4mg, Sodium: 124mg, Fiber: 1g

Easy Raspberry Ice Cream

Makes 3 servings

> 8 ounces (1¾ cups) frozen unsweetened raspberries
> 2 to 3 tablespoons powdered sugar
> ½ cup whipping cream

1. Place raspberries in food processor fitted with steel blade. Process using on/off pulsing action about 15 seconds or until raspberries resemble coarse crumbs.

2. Add sugar; process using on/off pulsing action until smooth. With processor running, add cream, processing until well blended. Serve immediately.

Variation: Substitute other low-carb fruits such as strawberries for the raspberries.

Nutrients per Serving:
Calories: 193 (68% of calories from fat), Carbohydrate: 15g, Total Fat: 15g, Protein: 2g, Cholesterol: 54mg, Sodium: 15mg, Fiber: 3g

Chocolate Peanut Butter Ice Cream Sandwiches

Easy Fruit Tarts

Makes 12 servings

12 wonton skins
    Vegetable cooking spray
2 tablespoons apple jelly or apricot fruit spread
1½ cups sliced or cut-up fruit such as DOLE® Bananas, Strawberries or Red or Green
    Seedless Grapes
1 cup nonfat or low fat yogurt, any flavor

• Press wonton skins into 12 muffin cups sprayed with vegetable cooking spray, allowing corners to stand up over edges of muffin cups.

• Bake at 375°F 5 minutes or until lightly browned. Carefully remove wonton cups to wire rack; cool.

• Cook and stir jelly in small saucepan over low heat until jelly melts.

• Brush bottoms of cooled wonton cups with melted jelly. Place two fruit slices in each cup; spoon rounded tablespoon of yogurt on top of fruit. Garnish with fruit slice and mint leaves. Serve immediately.

Prep Time: 20 minutes
Bake Time: 5 minutes

Nutrients per Serving:
Calories: 57 (5% of calories from fat), Carbohydrate: 12g, Total Fat: <1g, Protein: 1g, Cholesterol: 2mg, Sodium: 32mg, Fiber: 1g

Frozen Berry Ice Cream

Makes 8 servings (½ cup each)

8 ounces frozen unsweetened strawberries, partially thawed
8 ounces frozen unsweetened peaches, partially thawed
4 ounces frozen unsweetened blueberries, partially thawed
6 packets sugar substitute
2 teaspoons vanilla
2 cups no-sugar-added light vanilla ice cream
16 blueberries
4 small strawberries, halved
8 peach slices

1. Combine frozen strawberries, peaches, blueberries, sugar substitute and vanilla in food processor. Process until coarsely chopped.

2. Add ice cream; process until well blended.

3. Serve immediately for semi-soft texture or freeze and allow to stand 10 minutes before serving. Garnish each serving with 2 blueberries, 1 strawberry half and 1 peach slice.

Nutrients per Serving:
Calories: 69 (2% of calories from fat), Carbohydrate: 15g, Total Fat: <1g, Protein: 3g, Cholesterol: 0mg, Sodium: 23mg, Fiber: 1g

Apricot and Toasted Almond Phyllo Cups

Makes 8 servings

   Nonstick butter-flavored cooking spray
½ cup low-fat (1%) cottage cheese
4 ounces reduced-fat cream cheese
2 packets sugar substitute *or* equivalent of 4 teaspoons sugar
1 tablespoon fat-free (skim) milk
¼ teaspoon vanilla
4 sheets phyllo dough
3 tablespoons apricot or blackberry preserves
¼ cup sliced almonds, toasted

1. Preheat oven 350°F. Coat 8 (2½-inch) muffin cups with cooking spray; set aside.

2. Beat cottage cheese, cream cheese, sugar substitute, milk and vanilla in large bowl at high speed of electric mixer until completely smooth; refrigerate until needed.

3. Place 1 sheet phyllo dough on work surface. Keep remaining sheets covered with plastic wrap and damp kitchen towel. Lightly spray phyllo sheet with cooking spray; top with another sheet; spray with cooking spray. Repeat with remaining sheets of phyllo.

4. Cut stack of phyllo into 8 pieces using sharp knife or kitchen scissors. Gently fit each stacked square into prepared muffin cup. Bake 5 minutes or until lightly browned; cool on wire rack.

5. Place preserves in small microwavable bowl. Microwave at HIGH (100%) 20 seconds or until just melted. Spoon 2 tablespoons cream cheese mixture into each phyllo cup; drizzle 1 teaspoon melted preserves on top of cheese mixture. Top with 1½ teaspoons almonds.

Nutrients per Serving:
Calories: 109 (41% of calories from fat), Carbohydrate: 12g, Total Fat: 5g, Protein: 5g, Cholesterol: 8mg, Sodium: 174mg, Fiber: 1g

Chocolate Flan

Makes 8 servings

 2 eggs, lightly beaten
24 packets NatraTaste® Brand Sugar Substitute
 2 heaping tablespoons unsweetened cocoa powder
 1 tablespoon cornstarch
 1 teaspoon almond extract
 1 (15-ounce) can evaporated skim milk
 1 cup fat-free milk

1. Preheat oven to 350°F. Coat a 3-cup mold with nonstick cooking spray.

2. In a medium bowl, whisk together eggs, NatraTaste®, cocoa, cornstarch and almond extract until smooth. Stir in evaporated milk and fat-free milk. Pour mixture into mold. Place mold in a baking pan. Pour enough water into the baking pan to reach halfway up sides of mold.*

3. Bake 2 hours. Mixture will not look completely set, but will become firm upon cooling. Let cool at room temperature 1 hour, then refrigerate for several hours. To serve, invert mold onto a plate, or spoon flan from the mold.

Baking mold in water helps cook the flan evenly without cracking.

Nutrients per Serving:
Calories: 82 (17% of calories from fat), Carbohydrate: 13g, Total Fat: 2g, Protein: 7g, Cholesterol: 56mg, Sodium: 93mg, Fiber: <1g

Cheese Blintzes with Strawberries & Sour Cream

Makes 4 servings

3 tablespoons melted butter, divided
1 container (15 ounces) whole-milk ricotta cheese
1 tablespoon plus 2 teaspoons powdered sugar substitute, divided
1 teaspoon vanilla
⅛ teaspoon ground nutmeg
8 (8-inch) prepared crêpes
½ cup sliced fresh strawberries
¼ cup sour cream

1. Preheat oven to 350°F. Brush 1 tablespoon butter over bottom of 13×9-inch baking dish.

2. Combine cheese, 1 tablespoon sugar substitute, vanilla and nutmeg in food processor; process until smooth. Spoon scant ¼ cup mixture onto center of each crêpe. Fold outside edges of crêpe over filling; roll up from bottom. Place crêpes, seam side down, in prepared dish. Brush with remaining 2 tablespoons butter. Bake uncovered 18 to 20 minutes or until hot.

3. Meanwhile, combine strawberries and remaining 2 teaspoons sugar substitute; set aside at room temperature. Transfer crêpes to serving plates; top with strawberries. Serve with sour cream.

Tip: Look for shelf-stable packages of crêpes near the berries in the supermarket produce section.

Nutrients per Serving:
Calories: 362 (67% of calories from fat), Carbohydrate: 16g, Total Fat: 27g, Protein: 15g, Cholesterol: 94mg, Sodium: 289mg, Fiber: <1g

Conversation Heart Cereal Treats

Makes 12 bars

> **2 tablespoons margarine or butter**
> **20 large marshmallows**
> **3 cups frosted oat cereal with marshmallow bits**
> **12 large conversation heart candies**

1. Line 8- or 9-inch square pan with aluminum foil, leaving 2-inch overhangs on 2 sides. Generously grease or spray with nonstick cooking spray.

2. Melt margarine and marshmallows in medium saucepan over medium heat 3 minutes or until melted and smooth, stirring constantly. Remove from heat.

3. Add cereal; stir until completely coated. Spread in prepared pan; press evenly onto bottom using greased rubber spatula. Press heart candies into top of treats while still warm, evenly spacing to allow 1 heart per bar. Let cool 10 minutes. Using foil overhangs as handles, remove treats from pan. Cut into 12 bars.

Nutrients per Serving:
Calories: 62 (29% of calories from fat), Carbohydrate: 11g, Total Fat: 2g, Protein: 1g, Cholesterol: 0mg, Sodium: 62mg, Fiber: <1g

White Chocolate Pudding Parfaits

Makes 4 servings

    1 package (4-serving size) sugar-free instant white chocolate pudding mix
    2 cups reduced-fat (2%) milk
    ¾ cup whipping cream
 1½ cups fresh raspberries or sliced strawberries
    2 tablespoons chopped roasted shelled pistachio nuts or chopped toasted
         macadamia nuts

1. Combine pudding mix and milk in medium bowl; beat with wire whisk or electric mixer 2 minutes. Refrigerate 5 minutes or until thickened. Beat whipping cream in small deep bowl at high speed of electric mixer until stiff peaks form. Fold whipped cream into pudding.

2. In each of 4 parfait or wine glasses, layer ¼ cup pudding and 2 tablespoons raspberries. Repeat layers. Spoon remaining pudding over berries. Serve immediately or cover and chill up to 6 hours before serving. Sprinkle with nuts just before serving.

Nutrients per Serving:
Calories: 284 (67% of calories from fat), Carbohydrate: 19g, Total Fat: 21g, Protein: 7g, Cholesterol: 71mg, Sodium: 291mg, Fiber: 4g

Food Fact

White chocolate is not really chocolate at all because it lacks chocolate liquor (the main component in unsweetened chocolate). White chocolate is cocoa butter with added sugar, milk and flavorings (often vanilla or vanillin) and is more delicate than other chocolates.

Lighter Than Air Chocolate Delight

Makes 8 servings

> 2 envelopes unflavored gelatin
> ½ cup cold water
> 1 cup boiling water
> 1⅓ cups nonfat dry milk powder
> ⅓ cup HERSHEY'S Cocoa or HERSHEY'S Dutch Processed Cocoa
> 1 tablespoon vanilla extract
> Dash salt
> Granulated sugar substitute to equal 14 teaspoons sugar
> 8 large ice cubes

1. Sprinkle gelatin over cold water in blender container; let stand 4 minutes to soften. Gently stir with rubber spatula, scraping gelatin particles off sides; add boiling water to gelatin mixture. Cover; blend until gelatin dissolves. Add milk powder, cocoa, vanilla and salt; blend on medium speed until well mixed. Add sugar substitute and ice cubes; blend on high speed until ice is crushed and mixture is smooth and fluffy.

2. Immediately pour into 4-cup mold. Cover; refrigerate until firm. Unmold onto serving plate.

Note: Eight individual dessert dishes may be used in place of 4-cup mold, if desired.

Nutrients per Serving:
Calories: 72 (5% of calories from fat), Carbohydrate: 10g, Total Fat: <1g, Protein: 6g, Cholesterol: 2mg, Sodium: 67mg, Fiber: 1g

Lime Sorbet

Makes 6 servings

> ½ cup fresh lime juice (about 4 limes)
> 1 tablespoon grated lime peel
> 1½ cups hot water
> 6 tablespoons sugar
> 1 egg white, lightly beaten
> 1 drop each green and yellow food color
> Mint leaves or citrus leaves (optional)

1. Combine juice and lime peel in medium bowl. Combine hot water and sugar in small bowl; stir to dissolve. Add sugar mixture, egg white and food color to juice mixture; pour into shallow pan. Cover; freeze until firm, stirring once an hour to break up ice crystals.

2. Remove sorbet from freezer about 20 minutes before serving. Garnish with mint, if desired.

Favorite recipe from The Sugar Association, Inc.

Nutrients per Serving:
Calories: 54 (0% of calories from fat), Carbohydrate: 14g, Total Fat: <1g, Protein: 1g, Cholesterol: 0mg, Sodium: 9mg, Fiber: 0g

Quick Chocolate Pudding
Makes 4 servings

¼ **cup unsweetened cocoa powder**
2 **tablespoons cornstarch**
1½ **cups reduced-fat (2%) milk**
6 to 8 **packets sugar substitute or equivalent of** ⅓ **cup sugar**
1 **teaspoon vanilla**
⅛ **teaspoon ground cinnamon (optional)**

1. Combine cocoa powder and cornstarch in medium microwavable bowl or 1-quart glass measure. Gradually whisk in milk until well blended.

2. Microwave at HIGH (100%) 2 minutes; stir. Microwave at MEDIUM-HIGH (70% power) 3 to 4½ minutes or until thickened, stirring every 1½ minutes.

3. Stir in sugar substitute, vanilla and cinnamon, if desired. Let stand at least 5 minutes before serving, stirring occasionally to prevent skin from forming. Serve warm or chilled.

Nutrients per Serving:
Calories: 78 (21% of calories from fat), Carbohydrate: 10g, Total Fat: 2g, Protein: 5g, Cholesterol: 7mg, Sodium: 56mg, Fiber: <1g

Raspberry Cheese Tarts

Makes 10 servings

Crust

1¼ cups graham cracker crumbs
5 tablespoons light margarine (50% less fat and calories)
¼ cup SPLENDA® Granular

Filling

4 ounces reduced-fat cream cheese
½ cup plain nonfat yogurt
1 cup SPLENDA® Granular
½ cup egg substitute
1 cup frozen raspberries

Crust

1. Preheat oven to 350°F. In medium bowl, mix together graham cracker crumbs, margarine, and ¼ cup SPLENDA®. Press about 1 tablespoon of crust mixture into 10 muffin pan cups lined with foil liners. Set aside.

Filling

2. In small bowl, beat cream cheese with electric mixer on low speed until soft, about 30 seconds. Add yogurt and beat on low speed until smooth, approximately 1 minute. Stir in SPLENDA® and egg substitute until well blended.

3. Place 1½ tablespoons raspberries (4 to 5) into each muffin cup. Divide filling evenly among muffin cups. Bake for 20 minutes or until firm.

4. Refrigerate for 2 hours before serving. Garnish as desired.

Nutrients per Serving:
Calories: 140 (43% of calories from fat), Carbohydrate: 15g, Total Fat: 6g, Protein: 5g, Cholesterol: 6mg, Sodium: 255mg, Fiber: 1g

Chocolate-Caramel S'Mores

Makes 6 servings

12 chocolate wafer cookies or chocolate graham cracker squares
2 tablespoons fat-free caramel topping
6 large marshmallows

1. Prepare coals for grilling. Place 6 wafer cookies top down on plate. Spread 1 teaspoon caramel topping in center of each wafer to within about ¼ inch of edge.

2. Spear 1 to 2 marshmallows onto long wood-handled skewer.* Hold several inches above coals 3 to 5 minutes or until marshmallows are golden and very soft, turning slowly. Push 1 marshmallow off into center of caramel. Top with plain wafer. Repeat with remaining marshmallows and wafers.

If wood-handled skewers are unavailable, use metal skewer and wear an oven mitt to protect hand from heat.

Tip: S'Mores, a favorite campfire treat, got their name because everyone who tasted them wanted "some more." In the unlikely event of leftover S'Mores, they can be reheated in the microwave at HIGH 15 to 30 seconds.

Nutrients per Serving:
Calories: 72 (23% of calories from fat), Carbohydrate: 14g, Total Fat: 2g, Protein: 1g, Cholesterol: 0mg, Sodium: 77mg, Fiber: 0g

Pineapple-Ginger Bavarian

Makes 5 servings

1 can (8 ounces) crushed pineapple in juice, drained and liquid reserved
1 package (4 serving size) sugar-free orange gelatin
1 cup sugar-free ginger ale
1 cup plain nonfat yogurt
¾ teaspoon grated fresh ginger
½ cup whipping cream
1 packet sugar substitute
¼ teaspoon vanilla

1. Combine reserved pineapple juice with enough water to equal ½ cup liquid. Pour into small saucepan. Bring to a boil over high heat.

2. Place gelatin in medium bowl. Add pineapple juice mixture; stir until gelatin is completely dissolved. Add ginger ale and half of crushed pineapple; stir until well blended. Add yogurt; whisk until well blended. Pour into 5 individual ramekins. Cover each ramekin with plastic wrap; refrigerate until firm.

3. Meanwhile, combine remaining half of pineapple and ginger in small bowl. Cover with plastic wrap; refrigerate.

4. Just before serving, beat cream in small deep bowl at high speed of electric mixer until soft peaks form. Add sugar substitute and vanilla; beat until stiff peaks form.

5. To serve, top each bavarian with 1 tablespoon whipped cream and 1 tablespoon pineapple mixture.

Tip: To save time, use 2 tablespoons ready-made whipped cream to garnish, if desired.

Nutrients per Serving:
Calories: 76 (12% of calories from fat), Carbohydrate: 12g, Total Fat: 1g, Protein: 4g, Cholesterol: 1mg, Sodium: 102mg, Fiber: <1g

Tempting Chocolate Mousse
Makes 6 servings

1 envelope unflavored gelatin
2½ cups nonfat milk
¼ cup HERSHEY₅S Cocoa or HERSHEY₅S Dutch Processed Cocoa
1 tablespoon cornstarch
1 egg yolk
1 teaspoon vanilla extract
Granulated sugar substitute to equal 8 teaspoons sugar
1 cup prepared sucrose-free whipped topping*

Prepare 1 envelope (1 ounce) sucrose-free dry whipped topping mix with $^1/_2$ cup very cold water according to package directions. (This makes about 2 cups topping; use 1 cup topping for mousse. Reserve remainder for garnish, if desired.)

1. Sprinkle gelatin over milk in medium saucepan; let stand 5 minutes to soften. Stir in cocoa, cornstarch and egg yolk; cook over medium heat, stirring constantly with whisk, until mixture comes to a boil. Reduce heat to low; cook, stirring constantly, until mixture thickens slightly, about 1 minute.

2. Remove from heat; cool to lukewarm. Stir in vanilla and sugar substitute. Pour mixture into medium bowl. Refrigerate, stirring occasionally, until thickened, about 45 minutes.

3. Fold 1 cup prepared whipped topping into chocolate mixture. Spoon into 6 individual dessert dishes. Cover; refrigerate until firm. Garnish with remaining whipped topping, if desired.

Nutrients per Serving:
Calories: 90 (30% of calories from fat), Carbohydrate: 11g, Total Fat: 3g, Protein: 9g, Cholesterol: 35mg, Sodium: 55mg, Fiber: 0g

Peach Custard

Makes 2 servings

½ **cup peeled fresh peach or nectarine chunks**
1 **can (5 ounces) evaporated fat-free milk***
¼ **cup cholesterol-free egg substitute** *or* **1 egg**
1 **packet sugar substitute** *or* **equivalent of 2 teaspoons sugar**
½ **teaspoon vanilla**
  Cinnamon

*If a 5-ounce can is not available, use ¹/₂ cup plus 2 tablespoons evaporated fat-free milk.

1. Preheat oven to 325°F. Divide peach chunks between two 6-ounce ovenproof custard cups. Whisk together milk, egg substitute, sugar substitute and vanilla. Pour mixture over peach chunks in custard cups.

2. Place custard cups in shallow 1-quart casserole. Carefully pour hot water into casserole to depth of 1-inch. Bake custards 50 minutes or until knife inserted in center comes out clean. Remove custard cups from water bath. Sprinkle with cinnamon; serve warm or at room temperature.

Note: Drained canned peach slices in juice may be substituted for fresh fruit.

Nutrients per Serving:
Calories: 52 (2% of calories from fat), Carbohydrate: 7g, Total Fat: <1g, Protein: 5g, Cholesterol: <1mg, Sodium: 71mg, Fiber: 1g

Chocolate-Almond Meringue Puffs

Makes 15 servings

  2 tablespoons granulated sugar
  3 packets sugar substitute
1½ teaspoons unsweetened cocoa powder
  2 egg whites, at room temperature
  ½ teaspoon vanilla
  ¼ teaspoon cream of tartar
  ¼ teaspoon almond extract
  ⅛ teaspoon salt
1½ ounces sliced almonds
  3 tablespoons sugar-free seedless raspberry fruit spread

1. Preheat oven to 275°F. Combine granulated sugar, sugar substitute and cocoa powder in small bowl; set aside.

2. Place egg whites in small bowl; beat at high speed of electric mixer until foamy. Add vanilla, cream of tartar, almond extract and salt; beat until soft peaks form. Add sugar mixture, 1 tablespoon at a time, beating until stiff peaks form.

3. Line baking sheet with foil. Spoon 15 equal mounds of egg white mixture onto foil. Sprinkle with almonds.

4. Bake 1 hour. Turn oven off but do not open door. Leave puffs in oven 2 hours longer or until completely dry. Remove from oven; cool completely.

5. Stir fruit spread and spoon about ½ teaspoon onto each meringue just before serving.

Tip: Puffs are best if eaten the same day they're made. If necessary, store in airtight container and add fruit topping at time of serving.

Nutrients per Serving:
Calories: 34 (26% of calories from fat), Carbohydrate: 4g, Total Fat: 1g, Protein: 1g, Cholesterol: 0mg, Sodium: 27mg, Fiber: <1g

Fruit Freezies

Makes 12 servings

1½ **cups (12 ounces) canned or thawed frozen peach slices, drained**
¾ **cup peach nectar**
1 **tablespoon sugar**
¼ **to** ½ **teaspoon coconut extract (optional)**

1. Place peaches, nectar, sugar and extract in food processor or blender container; process until smooth.

2. Spoon 2 tablespoons fruit mixture into each section of ice cube tray.*

3. Freeze until almost firm. Insert frill pick into each cube; freeze until firm.

Or, pour ⅓ cup fruit mixture into each of 8 plastic pop molds or small paper or plastic cups. Freeze until almost firm. Insert wooden stick into each mold; freeze until firm.

Apricot Freezies: Substitute canned apricot halves for peach slices and apricot nectar for peach nectar.

Pear Freezies: Substitute canned pear slices for peach slices, pear nectar for peach nectar and almond extract for coconut extract.

Pineapple Freezies: Substitute crushed pineapple for peach slices and unsweetened pineapple juice for peach nectar.

Mango Freezies: Substitute chopped fresh mango for canned peach slices and mango nectar for peach nectar. Omit coconut extract.

Nutrients per Serving:
Calories: 19 (1% of calories from fat), Carbohydrate: 5g, Total Fat: <1g, Protein: <1g, Cholesterol: 0mg, Sodium: 2mg, Fiber: <1g

Strawberry Bavarian Deluxe

Makes 10 servings

½ bag whole frozen unsweetened strawberries (1 mounded quart), partially thawed
¼ cup granular sucralose
¼ cup low-sugar strawberry preserves
¾ cup water, divided
2 tablespoons balsamic vinegar
2 envelopes (7 grams each) unflavored gelatin
1 tablespoon honey
½ cup pasteurized liquid egg whites or 4 egg whites*
½ teaspoon cream of tartar
1 teaspoon vanilla
1 pint strawberries
1 cup thawed frozen light whipped topping
　　Mint sprigs (optional)

Use clean, grade A uncracked eggs.

1. Chill a 2-quart nonstick Bundt Pan or other mold in freezer. Place strawberries, sucralose and preserves in food processor fitted with steel blade; process until smooth. Transfer mixture to bowl. Set aside.

2. Combine ¼ cup water and vinegar in small saucepan. Sprinkle in gelatin and let stand until softened, about 5 minutes. Stir in remaining ½ cup water and honey. Cook and stir over medium heat until gelatin dissolves.

3. Whisk gelatin mixture into berry mixture in bowl. Cover; refrigerate until mixture is soupy but not set.

4. Meanwhile, combine liquid egg whites and cream of tartar in bowl. When berry-gelatin mixture is soupy, beat egg white mixture and vanilla until soft peaks form.

5. Gently fold egg whites, ⅓ at a time, into chilled gelatin mixture until mixture is evenly colored. Pour mousse into prepared mold. Refrigerate for at least 8 hours or overnight.

6. Run knife tip around top of mold. Dip mold briefly into large bowl of hot water to loosen. To unmold, center flat serving plate on top of mold and, holding firmly so mold does not shift,

continued on page 294

Strawberry Bavarian Deluxe

Strawberry Bavarian Deluxe, continued

invert plate and mold. Shake gently to release. Remove mold and refrigerate 10 to 15 minutes. Garnish with mint sprigs, if desired. Cut into wedges; serve with fresh strawberries and whipped topping.

Nutrients per Serving:
Calories: 82 (14% of calories from fat), Carbohydrate: 15g, Total Fat: 1g, Protein: 3g, Cholesterol: 0mg, Sodium: 25mg, Fiber: 2g

Papa's Pecan Tassies

Makes 10 servings

> 1 purchased refrigerated unbaked 9-inch pie crust
> ½ cup SPLENDA® Granular
> 2 tablespoons cornstarch
> 1 egg *or* ¼ cup egg substitute
> ¾ cup water
> 1 tablespoon vanilla extract
> ½ cup chopped pecans

Preheat oven to 350°F. Unfold pie crust. Using a 2½-inch biscuit cutter, cut into 12 circles. Press dough scraps together and cut out 8 more circles for a total of 20 circles. Pat pastry circles into miniature muffin (or tassie) cups. Press to form tarts. In a medium saucepan, combine SPLENDA® Granular, cornstarch, egg, and water. Cook over medium heat until mixture thickens and starts to boil, stirring constantly. Remove from heat. Stir in vanilla extract and pecans. Evenly spoon about 1 tablespoon mixture into each tart. Bake for 16 to 20 minutes. Place muffin pans on a wire rack and allow to cool for 10 minutes. Remove tassies from pans and continue cooling on wire rack.

Nutrients per Serving:
Calories: 155 (58% of calories from fat), Carbohydrate: 14g, Total Fat: 10g, Protein: 2g, Cholesterol: 25mg, Sodium: 88mg, Fiber: <1g

Chocolate Fondue with Fresh Fruit

Makes 8 servings

- 3 tablespoons unsweetened cocoa
- 1 cup heavy cream
- 4 ounces (½ cup) cream cheese, cut into chunks
- 3 tablespoons plus 1 teaspoon sucralose-based sugar substitute
- ½ teaspoon vanilla
- 24 green or red seedless grapes
- 12 small to medium strawberries, halved, or 6 large strawberries quartered

1. Combine cocoa and ½ cup cream in small saucepan or fondue pot over low heat. Whisk until well blended. When mixture is hot and thick, add remaining ½ cup cream and cream cheese. Cook, stirring constantly, until mixture is smooth and thick. Stir in sucralose and vanilla.

2. Keep warm over very low heat. Arrange grapes and strawberries on a plate. Use 7-inch-long wooden skewers or fondue forks for dipping.

Tip: Substitute in-season fruit for the grapes and strawberries.

Nutrients per Serving:
Calories: 177 (80% of calories from fat), Carbohydrate: 7g, Total Fat: 16g, Protein: 2g, Cholesterol: 57mg, Sodium: 55mg, Fiber: 1g

Speedy Pineapple-Lime Sorbet

Makes 8 servings

1 ripe pineapple, cut into cubes (about 4 cups)
⅓ cup frozen limeade concentrate, thawed
1 to 2 tablespoons fresh lime juice
1 teaspoon grated lime peel

1. Arrange pineapple in single layer on large baking pan; freeze 1 hour or until very firm. If desired, freeze pineapple up to 1 month in resealable plastic freezer food storage bags.

2. Combine frozen pineapple, limeade, lime juice and lime peel in food processor; process until smooth and fluffy. If pineapple doesn't become smooth and fluffy, let stand 30 minutes to soften slightly; repeat processing. Garnish as desired. Serve immediately.

Note: This dessert is best if served immediately, but it may be made ahead, stored in the freezer and softened before serving.

Nutrients per Serving:
Calories: 56 (5% of calories from fat), Carbohydrate: 15g, Total Fat: <1g, Protein: <1g, Cholesterol: 0mg, Sodium: 1mg, Fiber: 1g

Waist-Watcher's Cocoa Dessert

Makes 6 servings

　1 envelope unflavored gelatin
1¾ cups cold water
　⅔ cup nonfat dry milk powder
　2 egg yolks, slightly beaten
　3 tablespoons HERSHEY'S Cocoa
　¼ teaspoon salt
　½ cup sugar or equivalent amount of granulated sugar substitute
　2 teaspoons vanilla extract
　½ cup frozen light non-dairy whipped topping, thawed
　　Assorted fresh fruit, cut up (optional)
　　Additional frozen light non-dairy whipped topping, thawed (optional)
　　Additional HERSHEY'S Cocoa (optional)

1. Sprinkle gelatin over water in medium saucepan; let stand 5 minutes to soften. Add milk powder, egg yolks, 3 tablespoons cocoa and salt. Cook over medium heat, stirring constantly, until mixture begins to boil; remove from heat. Stir in sugar and vanilla. Pour mixture into large bowl. Refrigerate, stirring occasionally, until mixture mounds slightly when dropped from spoon, about 1 hour.

2. Fold ½ cup whipped topping into chocolate mixture. Pour into 6 individual dessert dishes. Cover; refrigerate until firm, about 4 hours. Garnish individual dessert dishes with assorted fresh fruit or additional whipped topping, sprinkled with additional cocoa, if desired.

Note: A 3-cup mold may be used in place of individual dessert dishes, if desired.

Nutrients per Serving:
Calories: 93 (27% of calories from fat), Carbohydrate: 11g, Total Fat: 3g, Protein: 5g, Cholesterol: 72mg, Sodium: 144mg, Fiber: 1g

Three-Melon Soup

Makes 4 servings

> 3 cups cubed, seeded watermelon
> 3 tablespoons unsweetened pineapple juice
> 2 tablespoons lemon juice
> ¼ cantaloupe melon
> ⅛ honeydew melon

1. Combine watermelon, pineapple juice and lemon juice in blender; process until smooth. Chill at least 2 hours or overnight.

2. Scoop out balls of cantaloupe and honeydew.

3. To serve, pour watermelon mixture into shallow bowls; garnish with cantaloupe and honeydew.

Nutrients per Serving:
Calories: 68 (8% of calories from fat), Carbohydrate: 16g, Total Fat: 1g, Protein: 1g, Cholesterol: 0mg, Sodium: 9mg, Fiber: 1g

Chocolate-Peanut Butter-Apple Treats

Makes 8 servings

> ½ (8-ounce) package fat-free or reduced-fat cream cheese, softened
> ¼ cup reduced-fat chunky peanut butter
> 2 tablespoons mini chocolate chips
> 2 large apples

1. Combine cream cheese, peanut butter and chocolate chips in a small bowl; mix well.

2. Cut each apple into 12 wedges; discard stems and seeds. Spread about 1½ teaspoons of the mixture over each apple slice.

Nutrients per Serving:
Calories: 101 (37% of calories from fat), Carbohydrate: 12g, Total Fat: 4g, Protein: 4g, Cholesterol: 2mg, Sodium: 144mg, Fiber: 2g

Three-Melon Soup

Tapioca Pudding

Makes 6 servings

2¾ cups low-fat milk
½ cup SPLENDA® Granular
¼ cup egg substitute
3 tablespoons quick-cooking tapioca
⅛ teaspoon salt
1½ teaspoons vanilla

1. In large saucepan, combine milk, SPLENDA®, egg substitute, tapioca and salt. Stir until blended, about 30 seconds. Let stand for 5 minutes.

2. Heat over medium heat, stirring constantly, until pudding comes to a full boil.

3. Remove from heat and stir in vanilla. Cool at room temperature for 20 minutes. Stir once and serve.

Preparation Time: 25 minutes
Cooking Time: 15 minutes

Nutrients per Serving:
Calories: 92 (24% of calories from fat), Carbohydrate: 12g, Total Fat: 2g, Protein: 5g, Cholesterol: 9mg, Sodium: 125mg, Fiber: <1g

Pears with Strawberry Sweet Dipping Cream

Makes 8 servings

4 ounces fresh or thawed frozen unsweetened strawberries
¼ cup reduced-fat cream cheese
¼ cup nonfat plain yogurt
2 packets sugar substitute
½ teaspoon vanilla
2 medium pears, cut into ½-inch slices

1. Process strawberries in food processor or blender until coarsely chopped. Add cream cheese, yogurt, sugar substitute and vanilla. Cover and process until smooth.

2. To serve, dip pear slices in cream cheese mixture.

Nutrients per Serving:
Calories: 52 (25% of calories from fat), Carbohydrate: 8g, Total Fat: 1g, Protein: 2g, Cholesterol: 4mg, Sodium: 43mg, Fiber: 1g

Cherry-Peach Pops

Makes 7 servings

⅓ cup peach nectar or apricot nectar
1 teaspoon unflavored gelatin
1 (15-ounce) can sliced peaches in light syrup, drained
1 (6- or 8-ounce) carton fat-free, sugar-free peach or cherry yogurt
1 (6- or 8-ounce) carton fat-free, sugar-free cherry yogurt

1. Combine nectar and unflavored gelatin in small saucepan; let stand 5 minutes. Stir over low heat just until gelatin dissolves.

2. Combine nectar mixture, drained peaches and yogurts in food processor. Cover and process until smooth.

3. Pour into 7 (3-ounce) paper cups, filling each about ⅔ full. Place in freezer; freeze 1 hour. Insert wooden stick into center of each cup. Freeze at least 3 hours.

4. Let stand at room temperature 10 minutes before serving. Tear away paper cups to serve.

Nutrients per Serving:
Calories: 52 (1% of calories from fat), Carbohydrate: 11g, Total Fat: <1g, Protein: 2g, Cholesterol: 1mg, Sodium: 34mg, Fiber: <1g

Café au Lait Ice Cream Sundaes

Makes 4 servings

3 cups whipping cream, divided
4 egg yolks, lightly beaten
1 tablespoon instant coffee granules
½ cup plus 2 tablespoons no-calorie sugar substitute for baking, divided
½ teaspoon vanilla
½ cup chopped walnuts or pecans

1. Pour 2 cups cream into medium saucepan. Whisk egg yolks and coffee granules into cream. Heat 10 minutes over low heat, stirring constantly, until mixture reaches 160°F and is thickened slightly.

2. Pour mixture into bowl; stir in ½ cup sugar substitute until well blended. Refrigerate 2 to 3 hours or until cold. Pour chilled mixture into ice cream maker; freeze according to manufacturer's directions.

3. Beat remaining 1 cup cream, 2 tablespoons sugar substitute and vanilla at high speed of electric mixer until stiff peaks form. Scoop ice cream into serving bowls; top with whipped cream. Sprinkle with nuts just before serving.

Tip: The ice cream will become harder the longer it is stored in freezer, so it is best eaten when freshly made.

Nutrients per Serving:
Calories: 798 (92% of calories from fat), Carbohydrate: 12g, Total Fat: 82g, Protein: 9g, Cholesterol: 459mg, Sodium: 79mg, Fiber: 1g

Café au Lait Ice Cream Sundae

Strawberry-Topped Cheesecake Cups

Makes 8 servings

  1 cup sliced strawberries
 10 packages sugar substitute, divided
  1 teaspoon vanilla, divided
 ½ teaspoon grated orange peel
 ¼ teaspoon grated fresh ginger
  1 package (8 ounces) cream cheese, softened
 ½ cup sour cream
  2 tablespoons granulated sugar
 16 vanilla wafers, crushed

1. Combine strawberries, 1 package sugar substitute, ¼ teaspoon vanilla, orange peel and ginger in medium bowl; toss gently. Let stand 20 minutes to allow flavors to blend.

2. Meanwhile, combine cream cheese, sour cream, remaining 9 packets sugar substitute and granulated sugar in medium bowl. Add remaining ¾ teaspoon vanilla; beat 30 seconds at low speed of electric mixer. Increase to medium speed; beat 30 seconds or until smooth.

3. Spoon cream cheese mixture into 8 individual ¼-cup ramekins. Top each with about 2 tablespoons vanilla wafer crumbs and about 2 tablespoons strawberry mixture.

Nutrients per Serving:
Calories: 205 (66% of calories from fat), Carbohydrate: 15g, Total Fat: 15g, Protein: 3g, Cholesterol: 36mg, Sodium: 127mg, Fiber: <1g

Choco-Orange Fluff

Makes 8 servings

⅓ **cup sugar**
¼ **cup HERSHEY'S Cocoa**
1 **envelope unflavored gelatin**
2 **cups nonfat milk**
1 **teaspoon vanilla extract**
⅛ **to** ¼ **teaspoon orange extract**
1½ **cups frozen light non-dairy whipped topping, thawed**
    Additional frozen light non-dairy whipped topping, thawed (optional)
    Fresh orange wedges (optional)

1. Stir together sugar, cocoa and gelatin in medium saucepan. Stir in milk; let stand 2 minutes to soften gelatin.

2. Cook over medium heat, stirring constantly, until gelatin is completely dissolved, about 5 minutes.

3. Pour mixture into medium bowl; stir in vanilla and orange extract. Refrigerate, stirring occasionally, until mixture mounds slightly when dropped from spoon (do not allow to gel).

4. Add 1½ cups whipped topping to chocolate mixture; beat with whisk until well blended. Refrigerate about 10 minutes to thicken slightly.

5. Spoon into 8 individual dessert dishes. Cover; refrigerate until firm, 3 to 4 hours. Garnish with additional whipped topping and orange wedges, if desired.

Nutrients per Serving:
Calories: 97 (18% of calories from fat), Carbohydrate: 16g, Total Fat: 2g, Protein: 3g, Cholesterol: 1mg, Sodium: 34mg, Fiber: 1g

Cranberry-Orange Bread Pudding

Makes 9 servings

  2 cups cubed cinnamon bread
¼ cup dried cranberries
  2 cups low-fat (1%) milk
  1 package (4-serving size) sugar-free vanilla pudding and pie filling mix*
½ cup cholesterol-free egg substitute *or* 2 eggs
  1 teaspoon grated orange peel
  1 teaspoon vanilla
½ teaspoon ground cinnamon
    Low-fat no-sugar-added vanilla ice cream (optional)

*Do not use instant pudding and pie filling.

1. Preheat oven to 325°F. Spray 9 custard cups with nonstick cooking spray.

2. Evenly divide bread cubes among custard cups. Bake 10 minutes; add cranberries.

3. Combine remaining ingredients except ice cream in medium bowl. Carefully pour over mixture in custard cups. Let stand 5 to 10 minutes.

4. Place cups on baking sheet; bake 25 to 30 minutes or until centers are almost set. Let stand 10 minutes. Serve with ice cream, if desired.

Nutrients per Serving:
Calories: 67 (13% of calories from fat), Carbohydrate: 11g, Total Fat: 1g, Protein: 4g, Cholesterol: 2mg, Sodium: 190mg, Fiber: <1g

Cookies

Pfeffernüsse

Makes about 5 dozen cookies (1 cookie per serving)

3½ cups all-purpose flour
  2 teaspoons baking powder
1½ teaspoons ground cinnamon
  1 teaspoon ground ginger
  ½ teaspoon baking soda
  ½ teaspoon salt
  ½ teaspoon ground cloves
  ½ teaspoon ground cardamom
  ¼ teaspoon black pepper
  1 cup (2 sticks) butter, softened
  1 cup granulated sugar
  ¼ cup dark molasses
  1 egg
    Powdered sugar

1. Combine flour, baking powder, cinnamon, ginger, baking soda, salt, cloves, cardamom and pepper in large bowl.

2. Beat butter and sugar in large bowl with electric mixer at medium speed until light and fluffy. Beat in molasses and egg. Gradually add flour mixture. Beat at low speed until dough forms. Shape dough into disc; wrap in plastic wrap and refrigerate until firm, 30 minutes or up to 3 days.

3. Preheat oven to 350°F. Grease cookie sheets. Shape dough into 1-inch balls. Place 2 inches apart on prepared cookie sheets.

4. Bake 12 to 14 minutes or until golden brown. Transfer cookies to wire racks; dust with sifted powdered sugar. Cool completely. Store tightly covered at room temperature or freeze up to 3 months.

Nutrients per Serving:
Calories: 71 (42% of calories from fat), Carbohydrate: 10g, Total Fat: 3g, Protein: 1g, Cholesterol: 12mg, Sodium: 73mg, Fiber: <1g

Mocha Crinkles

Makes about 6 dozen cookies (1 cookie per serving)

1⅓ **cups packed light brown sugar**
½ **cup vegetable oil**
¼ **cup reduced-fat sour cream**
1 **egg**
1 **teaspoon vanilla**
1¾ **cups all-purpose flour**
¾ **cup unsweetened cocoa powder**
2 **teaspoons instant espresso or coffee granules**
1 **teaspoon baking soda**
¼ **teaspoon salt**
⅛ **teaspoon black pepper**
½ **cup powdered sugar**

1. Beat brown sugar and oil in medium bowl at medium speed of electric mixer. Add sour cream, egg and vanilla; beat until well blended. Set aside.

2. Combine flour, cocoa, espresso, baking soda, salt and pepper in separate medium bowl.

3. Add flour mixture to brown sugar mixture; mix well. Refrigerate dough until firm, 3 to 4 hours.

4. Preheat oven to 350°F. Pour powdered sugar into shallow bowl. Set aside. Shape dough into 1-inch balls. Roll balls in powdered sugar.

5. Bake on ungreased cookie sheets 10 to 12 minutes or until tops of cookies are firm. *Do not overbake.* Cool on wire racks.

Nutrients per Serving:
Calories: 44 (30% of calories from fat), Carbohydrate: 7g, Total Fat: 1g, Protein: 0g, Cholesterol: 3mg, Sodium: 28mg, Fiber: 0g

Lemony Butter Cookies

Makes about 2½ dozen cookies (1 cookie per serving)

> ½ **cup (1 stick) butter, softened**
> ½ **cup sugar**
> 1 **egg**
> 1½ **cups all-purpose flour**
> 2 **tablespoons fresh lemon juice**
> 1 **teaspoon grated lemon peel**
> ½ **teaspoon baking powder**
> ⅛ **teaspoon salt**
>   **Additional sugar**

1. Beat butter and sugar in large bowl at medium speed of electric mixer until creamy. Beat in egg until light and fluffy. Mix in flour, lemon juice, lemon peel, baking powder and salt. Wrap dough in plastic wrap; refrigerate about 2 hours or until firm.

2. Preheat oven to 350°F. Roll out dough, a small portion at a time, on well-floured surface to ¼-inch thickness. (Keep remaining dough in refrigerator.) Cut with 3-inch round or fluted cookie cutter. Transfer to ungreased cookie sheets. Sprinkle with sugar.

3. Bake 8 to 10 minutes or until edges are lightly browned. Cool 1 minute on cookie sheets. Remove to wire racks; cool completely. Store in airtight container.

Nutrients per Serving:
Calories: 67 (47% of calories from fat), Carbohydrate: 8g, Total Fat: 3g, Protein: 1g, Cholesterol: 16mg, Sodium: 53mg, Fiber: <1g

Festive Fudge Blossoms

Makes 4 dozen cookies (1 cookie per serving)

¼ cup (½ stick) butter, softened
1 box (18.25 ounces) chocolate fudge cake mix
1 egg, lightly beaten
2 tablespoons water
¾ to 1 cup finely chopped walnuts
48 chocolate star candies

1. Preheat oven to 350°F. Cut butter into cake mix in large bowl until mixture resembles coarse crumbs. Stir in egg and water until well blended.

2. Shape dough into ½-inch balls; roll in walnuts, pressing nuts gently into dough. Place about 2 inches apart on ungreased baking sheets.

3. Bake cookies 12 minutes or until puffed and nearly set. Place chocolate star in center of each cookie; bake 1 minute. Cool 2 minutes on baking sheets. Remove to wire racks; cool completely.

Nutrients per Serving:
Calories: 73 (49% of calories from fat), Carbohydrate: 10g, Total Fat: 4g, Protein: 1g, Cholesterol: 4mg, Sodium: 120mg, Fiber: <1g

Food Fact

To keep moist cookies soft, store them in a tightly covered container for a day or two with 2 or 3 thick apple slices. Remember to remove the apple slices at the end of the two- or three-day period. Apple slices may also be added to a storage container to soften stale or overbaked cookies.

Maple Walnut Meringues

Makes about 36 cookies (1 cookie per serving)

⅓ **cup powdered sugar**
½ **cup plus ⅓ cup ground walnuts, divided**
¾ **cup packed light brown sugar**
3 **egg whites, at room temperature**
   Dash salt
⅛ **teaspoon cream of tartar**
1 **teaspoon maple extract**

1. Place 1 oven rack in the top third of oven and 1 oven rack in the bottom third of oven; preheat oven to 300°F. Line 2 large cookie sheets with aluminum foil, shiny side up.

2. Stir powdered sugar and ½ cup walnuts with fork in medium bowl; set aside. Crumble brown sugar into small bowl; set aside.

3. Beat egg whites and salt in large bowl at high speed of electric mixer until foamy. Add cream of tartar; beat 30 seconds or until mixture forms soft peaks. Sprinkle brown sugar, 1 tablespoon at a time, over egg white mixture; beat at high speed until each addition is completely absorbed. Beat 2 to 3 minutes or until mixture forms stiff peaks. Beat in maple extract at low speed. Gently fold in walnut mixture.

4. Drop level tablespoonfuls of dough to form mounds about 1 inch apart on prepared cookie sheets. Sprinkle with remaining ⅓ cup ground walnuts. Bake 25 minutes or until cookies feel dry on surface but remain soft inside. (Rotate cookie sheets from top to bottom halfway through baking time.)

5. Slide foil with cookies onto wire racks; cool completely. Carefully remove cookies from foil. Store in airtight container with waxed paper between layers of cookies.

Nutrients per Serving:
Calories: 41 (44% of calories from fat), Carbohydrate: 6g, Total Fat: 2g, Protein: 1g, Cholesterol: 0mg, Sodium: 6mg, Fiber: <1g

Chocolate Chip Cookies

Makes about 6 dozen cookies (1 cookie per serving)

½ cup margarine, softened
1½ cups packed light brown sugar
2 egg whites
1 teaspoon vanilla
2½ cups all-purpose flour
1½ teaspoons baking soda
½ teaspoon salt
⅓ cup fat-free (skim) milk
¾ cup (4 ounces) semisweet chocolate chips
½ cup chopped pecans or walnuts (optional)

1. Preheat oven to 350°F. Spray cookie sheets with nonstick cooking spray.

2. Beat margarine and brown sugar in large bowl at medium speed of electric mixer until fluffy. Beat in egg whites and vanilla.

3. Combine flour, baking soda and salt in medium bowl. Add flour mixture to margarine mixture alternately with milk, ending with flour mixture. Stir in chocolate chips and pecans, if desired.

4. Drop dough by slightly rounded tablespoonfuls onto prepared cookie sheets. Bake about 10 minutes or until lightly browned. Cool on wire racks.

Nutrients per Serving:
Calories: 56 (26% of calories from fat), Carbohydrate: 10g, Total Fat: 2g, Protein: 1g, Cholesterol: 0mg, Sodium: 61mg, Fiber: 0g

Almond Biscotti

Makes 32 biscotti (1 cookie per serving)

¼ **cup finely chopped slivered almonds**
½ **cup sugar**
2 **tablespoons margarine**
4 **egg whites, lightly beaten**
2 **teaspoons almond extract**
2 **cups all-purpose flour**
2 **teaspoons baking powder**
¼ **teaspoon salt**

1. Preheat oven to 375°F. Place almonds in small baking pan. Bake 7 to 8 minutes or until golden brown. (Watch almonds carefully; they burn easily.) Set aside.

2. Beat sugar and margarine in medium bowl at medium speed of electric mixer until smooth. Add egg whites and almond extract; beat until well blended. Combine flour, baking powder and salt in large bowl; mix well. Stir egg white mixture and almonds into flour mixture until well blended.

3. Spray two 9×5-inch loaf pans with nonstick cooking spray. Evenly divide dough between prepared pans; spread dough evenly onto bottoms of pans with wet fingertips. Bake 15 minutes or until knife inserted in centers comes out clean. Remove from oven; turn out onto cutting board.

4. As soon as loaves are cool enough to handle, cut each loaf into 16 (½-inch-thick) slices. Place slices on baking sheets covered with parchment paper or sprayed with cooking spray. Bake 5 minutes; turn over. Bake 5 minutes more or until golden brown. Serve warm or cool completely and store in airtight container.

Nutrients per Serving:
Calories: 56 (21% of calories from fat), Carbohydrate: 9g, Total Fat: 1g, Protein: 1g, Cholesterol: 0mg, Sodium: 53mg, Fiber: <1g

Mexican Wedding Cookies

Makes about 4 dozen cookies (1 cookie per serving)

1 cup pecan pieces or halves
1 cup (2 sticks) butter, softened
2 cups powdered sugar, divided
2 cups all-purpose flour, divided
2 teaspoons vanilla
⅛ teaspoon salt

1. Place pecans in food processor. Process using on/off pulsing action until ground but not pasty.

2. Beat butter and ½ cup powdered sugar in large bowl at medium speed of electric mixer until light and fluffy. Gradually add 1 cup flour, vanilla and salt. Beat at low speed until well blended. Stir in remaining 1 cup flour and ground nuts with spoon. Shape dough into ball; wrap in plastic wrap and refrigerate 1 hour or until firm.

3. Preheat oven to 350°F. Shape dough into 1-inch balls. Place 1 inch apart on ungreased cookie sheets.

4. Bake 12 to 15 minutes or until pale golden brown. Let cookies stand on cookie sheets 2 minutes.

5. Meanwhile, place 1 cup powdered sugar in 13×9-inch glass dish. Transfer hot cookies to powdered sugar. Roll cookies in powdered sugar, coating well. Let cookies cool in sugar.

6. Sift remaining ½ cup powdered sugar over sugar-coated cookies before serving. Store tightly covered at room temperature or freeze up to 1 month.

Nutrients per Serving:
Calories: 90 (56% of calories from fat), Carbohydrate: 9g, Total Fat: 6g, Protein: 1g, Cholesterol: 11mg, Sodium: 12mg, Fiber: <1g

Flourless Peanut Butter Cookies

Makes about 2 dozen cookies (1 cookie per serving)

> **1 cup peanut butter**
> **1 cup packed light brown sugar**
> **1 egg**
> **24 milk chocolate candy stars or other solid milk chocolate candy**

Preheat oven to 350°F. Combine peanut butter, sugar and egg in medium bowl; beat until blended and smooth. Shape dough into 24 balls about 1½ inches in diameter. Place 2 inches apart on ungreased cookie sheets. Press one chocolate star on top of each cookie. Bake 10 to 12 minutes or until set. Remove to wire racks; cool completely.

Nutrients per Serving:
Calories: 62 (44% of calories from fat), Carbohydrate: 7g, Total Fat: 3g, Protein: 2g, Cholesterol: 5mg, Sodium: 30mg, Fiber: <1g

Chocolate Chip Macaroons

Makes about 3½ dozen cookies (1 cookie per serving)

> **2½ cups flaked coconut**
> **⅔ cup mini semisweet chocolate chips**
> **⅔ cup sweetened condensed milk**
> **1 teaspoon vanilla**

Preheat oven to 350°F. Grease cookie sheets. Combine coconut, chocolate chips, milk and vanilla in medium bowl; mix until well blended. Drop dough by rounded teaspoonfuls 2 inches apart onto prepared cookie sheets. Press dough gently with back of spoon to flatten slightly. Bake 10 to 12 minutes or until light golden brown. Let cookies stand on cookie sheets 1 minute. Remove to wire racks; cool completely.

Nutrients per Serving:
Calories: 49 (55% of calories from fat), Carbohydrate: 6g, Total Fat: 3g, Protein: 1g, Cholesterol: 2mg, Sodium: 7mg, Fiber: <1g

Refrigerator Cookies

Makes about 4 dozen cookies (1 cookie per serving [without decorations])

½ **cup sugar**
¼ **cup light corn syrup**
¼ **cup margarine, softened**
¼ **cup cholesterol-free egg substitute** *or* **1 egg**
 1 **teaspoon vanilla**
1¾ **cups all-purpose flour**
¼ **teaspoon baking soda**
¼ **teaspoon salt**
   Assorted cookie decorations (optional)

1. Beat sugar, corn syrup and margarine in large bowl. Add egg substitute and vanilla; mix well. Set aside.

2. Combine flour, baking soda and salt in medium bowl. Add to sugar mixture; mix well. Shape dough into 2 (1½-inch-wide) logs. Wrap in plastic wrap. Freeze 1 hour.

3. Preheat oven to 350°F. Line baking sheets with parchment paper. Cut dough into ¼-inch-thick slices; place 1 inch apart on prepared cookie sheets. Sprinkle with cookie decorations, if desired.

4. Bake 8 to 10 minutes or until edges are lightly browned. Cool on wire racks.

Variation: Add 2 tablespoons unsweetened cocoa powder to dough for chocolate cookies.

Nutrients per Serving:
Calories: 39 (23% of calories from fat), Carbohydrate: 7g, Total Fat: 1g, Protein: 0g, Cholesterol: 0mg, Sodium: 32mg, Fiber: 0g

Choco-Coco Pecan Crisps

Makes about 6 dozen cookies (1 cookie per serving)

½ cup (1 stick) butter, softened
1 cup packed light brown sugar
1 egg
1 teaspoon vanilla
1½ cups all-purpose flour
1 cup chopped pecans
⅓ cup unsweetened cocoa powder
½ teaspoon baking soda
1 cup flaked coconut

1. Beat butter and brown sugar in large bowl at medium speed of electric mixer until light and fluffy. Beat in egg and vanilla. Combine flour, pecans, cocoa and baking soda in small bowl until well blended. Add to creamed mixture, blending until stiff dough is formed.

2. Sprinkle coconut on work surface. Divide dough into 4 parts. Shape each part into roll about 1½ inches in diameter; roll in coconut until thickly coated. Wrap in plastic wrap; refrigerate until firm, at least 1 hour or up to 2 weeks. (For longer storage, freeze up to 6 weeks.)

3. Preheat oven to 350°F. Cut rolls into ⅛-inch-thick slices. Place 2 inches apart on ungreased cookie sheets. Bake 10 to 13 minutes or until firm and lightly browned. Remove to wire racks; cool completely.

Nutrients per Serving:
Calories: 49 (55% of calories from fat), Carbohydrate: 6g, Total Fat: 3g, Protein: 1g, Cholesterol: 6mg, Sodium: 24mg, Fiber: <1g

Macadamia Nut Crunchies

Makes 2 dozen cookies (1 cookie per serving)

1 egg, beaten
½ cup mashed ripe banana (about ½ medium banana)
⅓ cup butter or margarine, melted
¼ cup no-sugar-added pineapple fruit spread
1 teaspoon vanilla
1¼ cups all-purpose flour
⅓ cup unsweetened flaked coconut*
½ teaspoon baking powder
½ teaspoon salt
1 jar (3½ ounces) macadamia nuts, coarsely chopped (about ¾ cup)

Unsweetened flaked coconut is available in health food stores.

1. Preheat oven to 375°F. Combine egg, banana, butter, fruit spread and vanilla in medium bowl. Add flour, coconut, baking powder and salt; mix well. Stir in nuts.

2. Drop tablespoonfuls of dough 2 inches apart onto lightly greased cookie sheets. Bake 10 to 12 minutes or until lightly browned. Remove to wire racks; cool completely. Store in tightly covered container.

Nutrients per Serving:
Calories: 101 (55% of calories from fat), Carbohydrate: 10g, Total Fat: 6g, Protein: 1g, Cholesterol: 16mg, Sodium: 89mg, Fiber: 1g

Molded Scotch Shortbread

Makes 8 servings (1 wedge per serving)

1½ **cups all-purpose flour**
¼ **teaspoon salt**
¾ **cup (1½ sticks) butter, softened**
⅓ **cup sugar**
1 **egg**

1. Preheat oven to temperature recommended by shortbread mold manufacturer. Combine flour and salt in medium bowl.

2. Beat butter and sugar in large bowl at medium speed of electric mixer until light and fluffy. Beat in egg. Gradually add flour mixture. Beat at low speed until well blended.

3. Spray 10-inch ceramic shortbread mold with nonstick cooking spray. Press dough firmly into mold. Bake, cool and remove from mold according to manufacturer's directions.

Note: If shortbread mold is not available, preheat oven to 350°F. Shape tablespoonfuls of dough into 1-inch balls. Place 2 inches apart on ungreased cookie sheets; press with fork to flatten. Bake 18 to 20 minutes or until edges are lightly browned. Let cookies stand on cookie sheets 2 minutes; transfer to wire racks to cool completely. Makes 2 dozen cookies.

Nutrients per Serving:
Calories: 92 (59% of calories from fat), Carbohydrate: 9g, Total Fat: 6g, Protein: 1g, Cholesterol: 24mg, Sodium: 83mg, Fiber: <1g

Holiday Thumbprint Cookies

Makes 20 cookies (1 cookie per serving)

- 1 package (8 ounces) sugar-free low-fat yellow cake mix
- 3 tablespoons orange juice
- 2 teaspoons grated orange peel
- ½ teaspoon vanilla
- 5 teaspoons strawberry all-fruit spread
- 2 tablespoons pecans, chopped

1. Preheat oven to 350°F. Spray baking sheets with nonstick cooking spray.

2. Beat cake mix, orange juice, orange peel and vanilla in medium bowl at medium speed of electric mixer 2 minutes or until mixture looks crumbly. Increase speed and beat 2 minutes or until smooth dough forms. (Dough will be very sticky.)

3. Coat hands with nonstick cooking spray. Shape dough into 1-inch balls. Place balls 2½ inches apart on prepared baking sheets. Press center of each ball with thumb. Fill each thumbprint with ¼ teaspoon fruit spread. Sprinkle with nuts.

4. Bake 8 to 9 minutes or until cookies are light golden brown and no longer shiny. *Do not overbake.* Remove to wire racks; cool completely.

Nutrients per Serving:
Calories: 50 (20% of calories from fat), Carbohydrate: 10g, Total Fat: 1g, Protein: 1g, Cholesterol: 0mg, Sodium: 8mg, Fiber: 0g

Chocolate-Dipped Orange Logs

Makes about 3 dozen cookies (1 cookie per serving)

3¼ cups all-purpose flour
⅓ teaspoon salt
1 cup (2 sticks) butter, softened
1 cup sugar
2 eggs
1½ teaspoons grated orange peel
1 teaspoon vanilla
1 package (12 ounces) semisweet chocolate chips
1½ cups pecan pieces, finely chopped

1. Combine flour and salt in medium bowl. Beat butter in large bowl at medium speed of electric mixer until smooth. Gradually beat in sugar; increase speed to high and beat until light and fluffy. Beat in eggs, 1 at a time, blending well after each addition. Beat in orange peel and vanilla until blended. Gradually stir in flour mixture until blended. (Dough will be crumbly.)

2. Shape dough into disc; wrap in plastic wrap and refrigerate 2 hours or until firm. (Dough can be prepared one day in advance and refrigerated overnight.)

3. Preheat oven to 350°F. Shape dough into 1-inch balls. Roll balls on flat surface to form 3-inch logs about ½ inch thick. Place logs 1 inch apart on ungreased cookie sheets.

4. Bake 17 minutes or until bottoms of cookies are golden brown. (Cookies will feel soft and look white on top; they will become crisp when cool.) Transfer to wire racks to cool completely.

5. Melt chocolate chips in top of double boiler over hot, not boiling, water. Place chopped pecans on sheet of waxed paper. Dip one end of each cookie in chocolate, shaking off excess. Roll chocolate-covered ends in pecans. Place on waxed paper-lined cookie sheets and let stand until chocolate is set, or refrigerate about 5 minutes to set chocolate. Store in airtight container.

Nutrients per Serving:
Calories: 162 (56% of calories from fat), Carbohydrate: 8g, Total Fat: 10g, Protein: 2g, Cholesterol: 23mg, Sodium: 17mg, Fiber: 1g

Oatmeal Almond Balls

Makes 24 servings (1 cookie per serving)

¼ **cup sliced almonds**
⅓ **cup honey**
2 **egg whites**
½ **teaspoon ground cinnamon**
⅛ **teaspoon salt**
1½ **cups uncooked quick oats**

1. Preheat oven to 350°F. Place almonds on cookie sheet; bake 8 to 10 minutes or until golden brown. Set aside. Do not turn off oven.

2. Combine honey, egg whites, cinnamon and salt in large bowl; mix well. Add oats and toasted almonds; mix well.

3. Drop by rounded teaspoonfuls onto ungreased cookie sheet. Bake 12 minutes or until lightly browned. Remove to wire rack to cool.

Cook's Tip: Store unopened packages of nuts in a cool, dark place. Store opened packages in an airtight container in the refrigerator for six months, or in the freezer for up to two years.

Nutrients per Serving:
Calories: 42 (19% of calories from fat), Carbohydrate: 7g, Total Fat: 1g, Protein: 1g, Cholesterol: 0mg, Sodium: 16mg, Fiber: 0g

Lip-Smacking Lemon Cookies

Makes about 4 dozen cookies (1 cookie per serving)

½ **cup (1 stick) butter, softened**
1 **cup sugar**
1 **egg**
2 **tablespoons lemon juice**
2 **teaspoons grated lemon peel**
2 **cups all-purpose flour**
1 **teaspoon baking powder**
⅛ **teaspoon salt**
   Dash ground nutmeg

1. Beat butter in large bowl at medium speed of electric mixer until smooth. Add sugar; beat until well blended. Add egg, lemon juice and peel; beat until well blended.

2. Combine flour, baking powder, salt and nutmeg in large bowl. Gradually add flour mixture to butter mixture at low speed, blending well after each addition.

3. Shape dough into 2 logs, each about 1½ inches in diameter and 6½ inches long. Wrap each log in plastic wrap. Refrigerate 2 to 3 hours or up to 3 days.

4. Preheat oven to 350°F. Grease cookie sheets. Cut logs into ¼-inch-thick slices; place 1 inch apart on cookie sheets.

5. Bake about 15 minutes or until edges are lightly browned. Transfer to wire rack to cool. Store in airtight container.

Nutrients per Serving:
Calories: 54 (33% of calories from fat), Carbohydrate: 8g, Total Fat: 2g, Protein: 1g, Cholesterol: 10mg, Sodium: 33mg, Fiber: <1g

Chocolate Chip Fudgie Cups

Makes 2 dozen cookies (1 cookie per serving)

Chocolate Chip Dough

- ⅓ **cup stick butter or margarine, softened**
- 1 **egg**
- 1 **teaspoon vanilla**
- ⅓ **cup EQUAL® SPOONFUL***
- ⅓ **cup firmly packed brown sugar**
- 1 **cup all-purpose flour**
- ½ **teaspoon baking soda**
- ¼ **teaspoon salt**
- ½ **cup mini semi-sweet chocolate chips**

Fudge Nut Filling

- 1 **cup EQUAL® SPOONFUL****
- ¾ **cup all-purpose flour**
- 6 **tablespoons unsweetened cocoa**
- ⅓ **cup chopped nuts**
- 1 **teaspoon baking powder**
- ¼ **teaspoon salt**
- ½ **cup unsweetened applesauce**
- 6 **tablespoons stick butter or margarine, softened**
- 2 **eggs**
- 1 **teaspoon vanilla**

*May substitute 8 packets Equal® sweetener.

**May substitute 24 packets Equal® sweetener.

• For Chocolate Chip Dough, beat ⅓ cup butter with electric mixer until fluffy. Beat in 1 egg and 1 teaspoon vanilla until blended. Mix in ⅓ cup Equal® Spoonful and brown sugar until combined. Combine 1 cup flour, baking soda, and ¼ teaspoon salt. Mix into butter mixture.

• Stir in chocolate chips. Form dough into circle about ½ inch thick. Wrap tightly in plastic wrap and freeze while preparing Fudge Nut Filling.

• For Fudge Nut Filling, combine 1 cup Equal® Spoonful, ¾ cup flour, cocoa, nuts, baking powder and ¼ teaspoon salt. Beat applesauce, 6 tablespoons butter, 2 eggs and 1 teaspoon vanilla until blended. Stir in combined flour mixture until well blended.

• Remove Chocolate Chip Dough from freezer. Spread approximately 1 rounded tablespoonful of dough in each of 24 mini-muffin pans. Fill each with Fudge Nut Filling to top of cup.

• Bake in preheated 350°F oven 15 to 18 minutes. Let cool in muffin pans about 5 minutes; remove and cool completely on wire racks. Store in airtight container at room temperature.

Nutrients per Serving:
Calories: 145 (56% of calories from fat), Carbohydrate: 14g, Total Fat: 9g, Protein: 2g, Cholesterol: 42mg, Sodium: 162mg, Fiber: 1g

Chewy Apple Moons

Makes 1½ dozen cookies (1 cookie per serving)

¾ **cup thawed frozen unsweetened apple juice concentrate**
½ **cup coarsely chopped dried apples**
2 **eggs**
¼ **cup butter, melted and cooled**
1 **teaspoon vanilla**
1¼ **cups all-purpose flour**
½ **teaspoon baking powder**
½ **teaspoon ground cinnamon**
¼ **teaspoon salt**
⅛ **teaspoon ground nutmeg**

Preheat oven to 350°F. Combine apple juice concentrate and apples; let stand 10 minutes. Beat eggs in medium bowl. Blend in concentrate mixture, butter and vanilla. Add remaining ingredients; mix well. Drop tablespoonfuls of dough 2 inches apart onto greased cookie sheets. Bake 10 to 12 minutes or until firm and golden brown. Cool on wire rack. Store in tightly covered container.

Nutrients per Serving:
Calories: 90 (33% of calories from fat), Carbohydrate: 13g, Total Fat: 3g, Protein: 1g, Cholesterol: 31mg, Sodium: 86mg, Fiber: <1g

Butterscotch Crispies

Makes 8½ dozen cookies (1 cookie per serving)

　2 cups sifted all-purpose flour
　1 teaspoon baking soda
　1 teaspoon salt
　½ cup margarine
2½ cups packed light brown sugar
　2 eggs
　1 teaspoon vanilla extract
　2 cups quick-cooking rolled oats
　2 cups puffed rice cereal
　½ cup chopped walnuts

Preheat oven to 350°F. Sift flour, baking soda and salt onto waxed paper. Cream margarine and brown sugar with electric mixer at medium speed in large bowl until fluffy. Beat in eggs, 1 at a time, until fluffy. Stir in vanilla.

Add flour mixture, ⅓ at a time, until well blended; stir in rolled oats, rice cereal and walnuts. Drop by teaspoonfuls, about 1 inch apart, onto large cookie sheets lightly sprayed with nonstick cooking spray. Bake 10 minutes or until cookies are firm and lightly golden. Remove to wire racks; cool.

Favorite recipe from The Sugar Association, Inc.

Nutrients per Serving:
Calories: 50 (26% of calories from fat), Carbohydrate: 9g, Total Fat: 1g, Protein: 1g, Cholesterol: 4mg, Sodium: 49mg, Fiber: <1g

Holiday Sugar Cookies

Makes about 3 dozen cookies (1 cookie per serving)

1 cup (2 sticks) butter, softened
¾ cup sugar
1 egg
2 cups all-purpose flour
1 teaspoon baking powder
¼ teaspoon salt
¼ teaspoon ground cinnamon
   Colored sprinkles or sugars (optional)

1. Beat butter and sugar in large bowl at medium speed of electric mixer until creamy. Add egg; beat until fluffy.

2. Stir in flour, baking powder, salt and cinnamon until well blended. Shape dough into ball; wrap in plastic wrap and flatten. Refrigerate about 2 hours or until firm.

3. Preheat oven to 350°F. Roll out dough, small portion at a time, to ¼-inch thickness on lightly floured surface with lightly floured rolling pin. (Keep remaining dough wrapped in refrigerator.)

4. Cut dough with 3-inch cookie cutters. Decorate with colored sprinkles or sugars, if desired. Transfer to ungreased cookie sheets.

5. Bake 7 to 9 minutes until edges are lightly browned. Let cookies stand on cookie sheets 1 minute; transfer to wire racks to cool completely. Store in airtight container.

Nutrients per Serving:
Calories: 88 (51% of calories from fat), Carbohydrate: 10g, Total Fat: 5g, Protein: 1g, Cholesterol: 20mg, Sodium: 77mg, Fiber: <1g

Slice 'n' Bake Ginger Wafers

Makes about 4½ dozen cookies (1 cookie per serving)

½ cup (1 stick) butter, softened
1 cup packed brown sugar
¼ cup light molasses
1 egg
2 teaspoons ground ginger
1 teaspoon grated orange peel
¼ teaspoon salt
¼ teaspoon ground cinnamon
¼ teaspoon ground cloves
2 cups all-purpose flour

1. Beat butter, sugar and molasses in large bowl until light and fluffy. Add egg, ginger, orange peel, salt, cinnamon and cloves; beat until well blended. Stir in flour until well blended. (Dough will be very stiff.)

2. Divide dough in half. Shape each half into 8×1½-inch log. Wrap logs in waxed paper or plastic wrap; refrigerate at least 5 hours or up to 3 days.

3. Preheat oven to 350°F. Cut dough into ¼-inch-thick slices. Place about 2 inches apart on ungreased baking sheets. Bake 12 to 14 minutes or until set. Remove to wire racks; cool completely.

Serving Suggestion: Dip half of each cookie in melted white chocolate, or drizzle cookies with a glaze of 1¼ cups powdered sugar and 2 tablespoons orange juice. Or, cut cookie dough into ⅛-inch-thick slices and bake. Sandwich melted caramel candy or peanut butter between cooled cookies.

Nutrients per Serving:
Calories: 53 (33% of calories from fat), Carbohydrate: 9g, Total Fat: 2g, Protein: 1g, Cholesterol: 4mg, Sodium: 33mg, Fiber: <1g

Almond Crescents

Makes about 3 dozen cookies (1 cookie per serving)

1 cup (2 sticks) butter, softened
⅓ cup granulated sugar
1¾ cups all-purpose flour
¼ cup cornstarch
1 teaspoon vanilla
1½ cups ground toasted almonds*
Chocolate Glaze (recipe follows) or powdered sugar

*To toast almonds, spread on cookie sheet. Bake at 325°F for 4 minutes or until fragrant and golden.

1. Preheat oven to 325°F. Beat butter and granulated sugar in large bowl until creamy. Mix in flour, cornstarch and vanilla. Stir in almonds. Shape tablespoonfuls of dough into crescents. Place 2 inches apart on ungreased cookie sheets.

2. Bake 22 to 25 minutes or until light brown. Cool 1 minute. Remove to wire racks; cool completely. Prepare Chocolate Glaze; drizzle over cookies. Allow chocolate to set; store in airtight container. Or sprinkle with powdered sugar before serving.

Chocolate Glaze: Place ½ cup semisweet chocolate chips and 1 tablespoon butter in small resealable plastic bag. Place bag in bowl of hot water for 2 to 3 minutes or until chocolate is softened. Dry with paper towel. Knead until chocolate mixture is smooth. Cut off very tiny corner of bag. Drizzle chocolate mixture over cookies.

Nutrients per Serving:
Calories: 123 (66% of calories from fat), Carbohydrate: 10g, Total Fat: 9g, Protein: 2g, Cholesterol: 15mg, Sodium: 56mg, Fiber: 1g

Peanut Butter & Banana Cookies

Makes 2 dozen cookies (1 cookie per serving)

¼ cup (½ stick) butter
½ cup mashed ripe banana
½ cup no-sugar-added natural peanut butter
¼ cup thawed frozen unsweetened apple juice concentrate
1 egg
1 teaspoon vanilla
1 cup all-purpose flour
½ teaspoon baking soda
¼ teaspoon salt
½ cup chopped salted peanuts
   Whole peanuts (optional)

1. Preheat oven to 375°F. Beat butter in large bowl at medium speed of electric mixer until creamy. Add banana and peanut butter; beat until smooth. Blend in apple juice concentrate, egg and vanilla. Beat in flour, baking soda and salt. Stir in peanuts.

2. Drop rounded tablespoonfuls of dough 2 inches apart onto lightly greased cookie sheets; top each with one peanut, if desired. Bake 8 minutes or until set. Cool completely on wire racks. Store in tightly covered container.

Nutrients per Serving:
Calories: 100 (53% of calories from fat), Carbohydrate: 9g, Total Fat: 6g, Protein: 3g, Cholesterol: 14mg, Sodium: 88mg, Fiber: 1g

Classic Refrigerator Sugar Cookies

Makes about 4 dozen cookies (1 cookie per serving)

1 cup (2 sticks) butter, softened
1 cup sugar
1 egg
1 teaspoon vanilla
2 cups all-purpose flour
2 teaspoons baking powder
   Dash nutmeg
¼ cup milk
½ cup colored sprinkles (optional)

1. Beat butter in large bowl at medium speed of electric mixer until smooth. Add sugar; beat until well blended. Add egg and vanilla; beat until well blended.

2. Combine flour, baking powder and nutmeg in medium bowl. Add flour mixture and milk alternately to butter mixture, beating at low speed after each addition until well blended.

3. Shape dough into 2 logs, each about 2 inches in diameter and 6 inches long. Roll logs in colored sprinkles, if desired, coating evenly (about ¼ cup sprinkles per roll). Or, leave logs plain and decorate cookies with melted chocolate after baking. Wrap each log in plastic wrap. Refrigerate 2 to 3 hours or overnight.

4. Preheat oven to 350°F. Grease cookie sheets. Cut logs into ¼-inch-thick slices; place 1 inch apart on prepared cookie sheets. (Keep unbaked logs and sliced cookies chilled until ready to bake.)

5. Bake 8 to 10 minutes or until edges are golden brown. Transfer to wire racks to cool.

Serving Suggestion: For chocolate-dipped cookies, melt 1 cup semisweet chocolate chips in small saucepan over low heat for every 24 cookies. Dip plain cookies in melted chocolate or drizzle chocolate over cookies with fork or spoon. Set cookies on wire racks until chocolate is set. Store in airtight container.

Nutrients per Serving:
Calories: 71 (51% of calories from fat), Carbohydrate: 8g, Total Fat: 4g, Protein: 1g, Cholesterol: 15mg, Sodium: 54mg, Fiber: <1g

Cowboy Cookies

Makes about 4 dozen cookies (1 cookie per serving)

½ **cup (1 stick) butter, softened**
½ **cup packed light brown sugar**
¼ **cup granulated sugar**
1 **egg**
1 **teaspoon vanilla**
1 **cup all-purpose flour**
2 **tablespoons unsweetened cocoa powder**
½ **teaspoon baking powder**
¼ **teaspoon baking soda**
1 **cup uncooked old-fashioned oats**
1 **cup (6 ounces) semisweet chocolate chips**
½ **cup golden raisins**
½ **cup chopped nuts**

1. Preheat oven to 375°F. Lightly grease cookie sheets or line with parchment paper.

2. Beat butter and sugars in large bowl at medium speed of electric mixer until blended. Add egg and vanilla; beat until fluffy. Combine flour, cocoa, baking powder and baking soda in small bowl; stir into butter mixture. Add oats, chocolate chips, raisins and nuts. Drop by rounded teaspoonfuls 2 inches apart onto prepared cookie sheets.

3. Bake 10 to 12 minutes or until edges are lightly browned. Remove to wire racks; cool completely.

Nutrients per Serving:
Calories: 74 (49% of calories from fat), Carbohydrate: 10g, Total Fat: 4g, Protein: 1g, Cholesterol: 10mg, Sodium: 32mg, Fiber: <1g

Nutty Spice Cookies

Makes about 5 dozen cookies (1 cookie per serving)

½ cup light molasses
⅓ cup sugar
¼ cup cholesterol-free egg substitute *or* 1 egg
¼ cup water
2 tablespoons canola or vegetable oil
2¼ cups all-purpose flour
1 teaspoon baking soda
1 teaspoon ground ginger
½ teaspoon ground nutmeg
½ teaspoon ground cinnamon
¼ teaspoon ground cloves
⅓ cup chopped walnuts

1. Stir molasses, sugar, egg substitute, water and oil in medium bowl until sugar is dissolved. Sift flour, baking soda, ginger, nutmeg, cinnamon and cloves into large bowl; stir to combine. Add molasses mixture; stir with wooden spoon until smooth. (Dough will be stiff.) Wrap dough in plastic wrap; refrigerate at least 2 hours or up to 2 days.

2. Preheat oven to 375°F. Spray cookie sheets lightly with nonstick cooking spray. Roll out dough into 12-inch square on floured surface. If dough cracks, press together. Sprinkle walnuts evenly over dough, pressing nuts into dough with fingers. Cut square into 8 lengthwise strips, and then 8 crosswise strips to form 64 squares.

3. Place cookies 1 inch apart on prepared cookie sheets. Bake, 1 sheet at a time, 8 minutes or until edges are lightly browned. Remove cookies to wire racks; cool completely. Store in airtight container.

Nutrients per Serving:
Calories: 34 (20% of calories from fat), Carbohydrate: 6g, Total Fat: 1g, Protein: 1g, Cholesterol: 0mg, Sodium: 15mg, Fiber: <1g

Chocolate Dunking Biscotti

Makes about 2 dozen biscotti (1 cookie per serving)

1⅓ cups all-purpose flour
⅓ cup unsweetened cocoa powder
1 teaspoon baking powder
½ teaspoon ground allspice
¼ teaspoon salt
¾ cup granulated sugar
2 large eggs, lightly beaten
½ teaspoon almond extract

Glaze (optional)

¼ cup powdered sugar
1 teaspoon water

Preheat oven to 350°F and coat baking sheet with cooking spray. Sift together flour, cocoa powder, baking powder, allspice and salt in small bowl. Whisk granulated sugar, eggs and almond extract in medium bowl. Add flour mixture and mix with hands to form dough. Dough will be dry yet sticky. Divide dough in half and form two logs about 2 inches wide and 12 inches long on baking sheet. Bake 25 to 30 minutes. Remove from oven and cut each log into ½-inch slices. Slices can be further dried by baking 10 more minutes at 300°F. If moister biscuits are desired, omit second baking. To glaze, blend powdered sugar and water; drizzle over top of biscotti with spoon.

Favorite recipe from The Sugar Association, Inc.

Nutrients per Serving:
Calories: 57 (16% of calories from fat), Carbohydrate: 12g, Total Fat: 1g, Protein: 1g, Cholesterol: 18mg, Sodium: 42mg, Fiber: 1g

Pumpkin Polka Dot Cookies

Makes about 4 dozen cookies (1 cookie per serving)

1¼ cups EQUAL® SPOONFUL*
½ cup stick butter or margarine, softened
3 tablespoons light molasses
1 cup canned pumpkin
1 egg
1½ teaspoons vanilla
1⅔ cups all-purpose flour
1 teaspoon baking powder
1¼ teaspoons ground cinnamon
½ teaspoon ground nutmeg
½ teaspoon ground ginger
½ teaspoon baking soda
¼ teaspoon salt
1 cup mini semi-sweet chocolate chips

*May substitute 30 packets Equal® sweetener.

• Beat Equal®, butter and molasses until well combined. Mix in pumpkin, egg and vanilla until blended. Gradually stir in combined flour, baking powder, spices, baking soda and salt until well blended. Stir in chocolate chips.

• Drop by teaspoonfuls onto baking sheet sprayed with nonstick cooking spray. Bake in preheated 350°F oven 11 to 13 minutes. Remove from baking sheet and cool completely on wire rack. Store at room temperature in airtight container up to 1 week.

Nutrients per Serving:
Calories: 63 (43% of calories from fat), Carbohydrate: 8g, Total Fat: 3g, Protein: 1g, Cholesterol: 10mg, Sodium: 69mg, Fiber: 1g

Spiced Wafers

Makes about 4 dozen cookies (1 cookie per serving)

½ cup (1 stick) butter, softened
1 cup sugar
1 egg
2 tablespoons milk
1 teaspoon vanilla
1¾ cups all-purpose flour
2 teaspoons baking powder
1 teaspoon ground cinnamon
½ teaspoon ground nutmeg
¼ teaspoon ground cloves
   Red colored sugar or red hot candies, for garnish (optional)

1. Beat butter in large bowl at medium speed of electric mixer until smooth. Add sugar; beat until well blended. Add egg, milk and vanilla; beat until well blended.

2. Combine flour, baking powder, cinnamon, nutmeg and cloves in large bowl. Gradually add flour mixture to butter mixture, blending well at low speed after each addition.

3. Shape dough into 2 logs, each about 2 inches in diameter and 6 inches long. Wrap each log in plastic wrap. Refrigerate 2 to 3 hours or overnight.

4. Preheat oven to 350°F. Grease cookie sheets. Cut logs into ¼-inch-thick slices; decorate with candies or colored sugar, if desired. (Or, leave plain and decorate with icing later.) Place 2 inches apart on prepared cookie sheets.

5. Bake 11 to 13 minutes or until edges are lightly browned. Transfer to wire racks to cool. Store in airtight container.

Nutrients per Serving:
Calories: 52 (35% of calories from fat), Carbohydrate: 8g, Total Fat: 2g, Protein: 1g, Cholesterol: 10mg, Sodium: 35mg, Fiber: <1g

Mexican Chocolate Macaroons

Makes 3 dozen cookies (1 cookie per serving)

1 package (8 ounces) semisweet baking chocolate, divided
1¾ cups plus ⅓ cup whole almonds, divided
¾ cup sugar
1 teaspoon ground cinnamon
1 teaspoon vanilla
2 egg whites

1. Preheat oven to 400°F. Grease baking sheets; set aside.

2. Place 5 squares chocolate in food processor; process until coarsely chopped. Add 1¾ cups almonds and sugar; process using on/off pulsing action until mixture is finely ground. Add cinnamon, vanilla and egg whites; process just until mixture forms moist dough.

3. Shape dough into 1-inch balls (dough will be sticky). Place 2 inches apart on prepared baking sheets. Press 1 almond on top of each cookie.

4. Bake 8 to 10 minutes or just until set. Cool 2 minutes on baking sheets. Remove to wire racks; cool completely.

5. Heat remaining 3 squares chocolate in small saucepan over very low heat until melted. Spoon chocolate into small resealable plastic food storage bag. Cut small corner from bottom of bag. Drizzle chocolate over cookies.

Tip: For longer storage, allow cookies to stand until chocolate drizzle is set. Store in airtight containers.

Nutrients per Serving:
Calories: 87 (52% of calories from fat), Carbohydrate: 9g, Total Fat: 5g, Protein: 2g, Cholesterol: 0mg, Sodium: 4mg, Fiber: 1g

366

Chocolate Chip Cookies
Makes about 2 dozen cookies (1 cookie per serving)

⅓ cup stick butter or margarine, softened
1 egg
1 teaspoon vanilla
⅓ cup EQUAL® SPOONFUL*
⅓ cup firmly packed light brown sugar
¾ cup all-purpose flour
½ teaspoon baking soda
¼ teaspoon salt
½ cup semi-sweet chocolate chips or mini chocolate chips

May substitute 8 packets Equal® sweetener.

• Beat butter with electric mixer until fluffy. Beat in egg and vanilla until blended. Mix in Equal® and brown sugar until combined.

• Combine flour, baking soda and salt. Mix into butter mixture until well blended. Stir in chocolate chips.

• Drop dough by rounded teaspoonfuls onto ungreased baking sheet. Bake in preheated 350°F oven 8 to 10 minutes or until light golden color. Remove from baking sheet and cool completely on wire rack.

Nutrients per Serving:
Calories: 67 (54% of calories from fat), Carbohydrate: 8g, Total Fat: 4g, Protein: 1g, Cholesterol: 16mg, Sodium: 80mg, Fiber: <1g

Acknowledgments

The publisher would like to thank the companies and organizations listed below for the use of their recipes and photographs in this publication.

Birds Eye®

Butterball® Turkey

Del Monte Corporation

Dole Food Company, Inc.

Equal® sweetener

Florida's Citrus Growers

Hershey Foods Corporation

Hormel Foods, LLC

The Kingsford Products Company

National Chicken Council / US Poultry & Egg Association

National Pork Board

NatraTaste® is a registered trademark of Stadt Corporation

Splenda® is a registered trademark of McNeil Nutritionals

StarKist® Seafood Company

The Sugar Association, Inc.

Uncle Ben's Inc.

Unilever Bestfoods North America

Index

376

Notes

Notes

METRIC CONVERSION CHART

VOLUME MEASUREMENTS (dry)

⅛ teaspoon = 0.5 mL
¼ teaspoon = 1 mL
½ teaspoon = 2 mL
¾ teaspoon = 4 mL
1 teaspoon = 5 mL
1 tablespoon = 15 mL
2 tablespoons = 30 mL
¼ cup = 60 mL
⅓ cup = 75 mL
½ cup = 125 mL
⅔ cup = 150 mL
¾ cup = 175 mL
1 cup = 250 mL
2 cups = 1 pint = 500 mL
3 cups = 750 mL
4 cups = 1 quart = 1 L

VOLUME MEASUREMENTS (fluid)

1 fluid ounce (2 tablespoons) = 30 mL
4 fluid ounces (½ cup) = 125 mL
8 fluid ounces (1 cup) = 250 mL
12 fluid ounces (1½ cups) = 375 mL
16 fluid ounces (2 cups) = 500 mL

WEIGHTS (mass)

½ ounce = 15 g
1 ounce = 30 g
3 ounces = 90 g
4 ounces = 120 g
8 ounces = 225 g
10 ounces = 285 g
12 ounces = 360 g
16 ounces = 1 pound = 450 g

DIMENSIONS

1/16 inch = 2 mm
⅛ inch = 3 mm
¼ inch = 6 mm
½ inch = 1.5 cm
¾ inch = 2 cm
1 inch = 2.5 cm

OVEN TEMPERATURES

250°F = 120°C
275°F = 140°C
300°F = 150°C
325°F = 160°C
350°F = 180°C
375°F = 190°C
400°F = 200°C
425°F = 220°C
450°F = 230°C

BAKING PAN SIZES

Utensil	Size in Inches/Quarts	Metric Volume	Size in Centimeters
Baking or Cake Pan (square or rectangular)	8×8×2	2 L	20×20×5
	9×9×2	2.5 L	23×23×5
	12×8×2	3 L	30×20×5
	13×9×2	3.5 L	33×23×5
Loaf Pan	8×4×3	1.5 L	20×10×7
	9×5×3	2 L	23×13×7
Round Layer Cake Pan	8×1½	1.2 L	20×4
	9×1½	1.5 L	23×4
Pie Plate	8×1¼	750 mL	20×3
	9×1¼	1 L	23×3
Baking Dish or Casserole	1 quart	1 L	—
	1½ quart	1.5 L	—
	2 quart	2 L	—